THE OFFICIAL

DOWNTON ABBEY

AFTERNOON TEA COOKBOOK

FOREWORD BY GARETH NEAME

weldon**owen**

TABLE *of* CONTENTS

MRS. PATMORE: *I've got tea for all of us,*
and a snack for you later on.

MASON: *You're an angel of mercy.*

~ SEASON 6, EPISODE 5

FOREWORD

Few customs are more iconic of England than the afternoon tea. Everything about it—the etiquette, the fine English china, the sandwiches and cakes—epitomizes some of the very best England has to offer.

Scenes of afternoon tea are prominently featured in *Downton Abbey*, all of them reflecting the height of fashion of the era. The word *'tea'* had long been used as an umbrella term for a variety of different occasions that involved tea drinking. It could be as modest as a cup of tea with a slice of cake at home or a pot of tea and some warm scones shared in a railway tearoom, or it could be a grand tea party held in the grounds of a great estate.

Downton Abbey gives the viewer a window into the tradition of this afternoon ritual both upstairs and downstairs. The servants' tea shows a rare moment of calm in the house, as the family upstairs can serve themselves as soon as the tea and food are displayed. Along with their cup of tea and a slice of bread or cake, the servants typically use the time to catch up on small tasks, such as mending a shirt and sewing on buttons. We see some footmen reading a newspaper, while others are lost in a book or sometimes playing cards.

For Violet, the Dowager Countess, afternoon tea visits are usually a moment for her to give grandmotherly advice or to meddle in family or village affairs. In season 3 episode 7, she summons Lady Edith to tea, during which she aims to convince her to look for a more suitable, lady-like occupation than becoming a columnist for *The Sketch*. Violet suggests running a charity or taking up watercolours. Edith listens, sips her tea, and then politely says she will take the job anyway.

Edith is breaking loose from the limitations that come with her social position as a woman from a great family. She symbolizes the modern times ahead in which women will not only gain more freedoms, but also the right to vote—a time when the corset and all it represents will finally be a thing of the past.

This little book is filled with recipes for many of the best offerings—biscuits and scones, cakes and tarts, savouries, preserves and more—that graced tea tables in the *Downton Abbey* era and continue to be enjoyed today. Just like the popular etiquette books of the time, these pages contain everything you need to know to organise your own proper afternoon tea.

GARETH NEAME
EXECUTIVE PRODUCER, *DOWNTON ABBEY* | LONDON, 2020

When the Portuguese princess Catherine of Braganza arrived in England in 1662 to marry Charles II, she carried among her belongings a chest of tea. With it she would change English drinking habits forever—or so the legend goes and has been repeated for more than 350 years. The story of the Queen's tea chest became a marketing tool for the exotic beverage at court and among the upper classes. It even prompted politician and lyric poet Edmund Waller to write "Of Tea, Commended by Her Majesty" in 1663 to honor Catherine's contribution. But tea was already available in England, as it had been introduced to Europe in the seventeenth century through trade with China. The Portuguese court had embraced a tea culture early on, and the beverage soon spread to the rest of Europe.

A decade before Catherine's marriage, the first coffeehouse opened in London, and soon they were everywhere, though only men were permitted to enter them. Thomas Garway (sometimes spelled "Garraway"), who owned a coffeehouse in London's Exchange Alley, began selling tea leaves and offering tea as a drink in 1657, reportedly the first purveyor in England to do so. He put together a pamphlet that explained this new beverage to his customers, detailing its Chinese origin, medical virtues, and popularity with "Persons of quality," namely those who could afford the commodity and the precious imported chinaware to go with it. It would be nearly one hundred years before the first English-made porcelain teapots were manufactured that could stand up to the heat of boiling water without shattering. By then, tea drinking had become commonplace.

THE KEY TO FEMALE EMPOWERMENT

In a domestic environment, tea was considered a family drink and good for the health—a cure for colds and fevers and other maladies. The mistress of the house was responsible for managing its consumption, just as she was responsible for preparing other medicinal potions. This arrangement was in stark contrast to public tea consumption in the male-only coffeehouses and in the pleasure gardens of London, where both sexes engaged in the scandalous practice of tea drinking.

The mistress of the house kept the key to the tea caddy as a sign of control, and in paintings of the time, the caddy is always placed closest to the dominant female of the party, indicating her role as lady of the house. That control did not change until the nineteenth century, when the responsibility of overseeing the tea caddy was ceded to the housekeeper.

In the eighteenth century, it was common for fashionable ladies to get together at one another's homes for tea and conversation. Before that time, they had little or no social freedom and were often isolated. The safety of a nonalcoholic drink gave them the opportunity to gather and socialize.

The first known tea shop in London was opened in 1706 by Thomas Twining, and although it was a male-only environment, ladies came in their carriages to the back entrance, where their servants would discreetly buy the tea for them. The shop stood at 216 Strand, where it remains to this day.

The Twining family played an even greater role in Britain's becoming a tea-drinking nation when Richard Twining, grandson of Thomas and head of the tea trade, lobbied Prime Minister William

Pitt to reduce the tax on tea. He reportedly argued that revenues would be greater if taxes were lowered. Fraud and smuggling would no longer be profitable, which would put an end to sellers adding sloe leaves or the like to make the tea stretch further. As a result of the efforts of Twining and others, the Commutation Act of 1784 passed, which dropped the tax rate from 119 percent to 12.5 percent, making tea widely affordable and effectively ending smuggling and adulteration. The law's passage also increased the profits of the British East India Company, of which Twining was a director.

TEA MEETINGS

The nineteenth-century Temperance movement aggressively promoted tea as an alternative to beer, and large tea meetings were organized and managed by women. Originally used for fundraising, these get-togethers quickly became about power. In his 1884 *Tea and Tea Drinking*, Arthur Reade writes that there was "a spirit of rivalry among the ladies as to who should have the richest and most elegantly furnished table." He illustrates a few occasions when six hundred to twelve hundred people sat down for tea and for "singing hinnies [griddlecakes], hot wigs [small buns], and spice loaf, served up in tempting display."

TEA AT HOME

The Duchess of Bedford is often credited with having invented afternoon tea in 1842. She reportedly was the first to request something to eat—small cakes, delicate sandwiches—along with a pot of tea to battle a "sinking feeling" in midafternoon. But afternoon tea was actually the result of an evolution in British dining culture. Until the late eighteenth century, dinner was eaten at what we today call lunchtime, and it was followed by supper, which was a much later and lighter meal. Tea in accompaniment with bread and butter was already part of eighteenth-century visiting rituals, as dinner started to move further into the afternoon. By the end of the nineteenth century, dinner had migrated to the evening,

creating an opportunity for the well-to-do to dress up for the occasion.

The word *tea* could mean several things in the Victorian and Edwardian periods. Low tea, or what would later become known as afternoon tea, was so-called because the tea and the refreshments—cakes, buns, pastries, sandwiches—were served on low tables rather than at the dining table. *High tea*, a term now often mistakenly confused with afternoon tea, was a hearty meal of meat pies and other savory dishes, breads, and cheese eaten by the working classes at dinnertime.

Village afternoon teas were another well-established custom. These carefully orchestrated events were organized by women of the upper class for the poor, often to celebrate a major royal event, such as Queen Victoria's Golden Jubilee in 1887 and Diamond Jubilee in 1897. Such gatherings not only fulfilled these women's need to be engaged in some kind of charitable work but also provided a way for everyone—the haves and the have-nots—to show their patriotism to Crown and country. This tradition, minus the strict class structure, has continued into the twenty-first century, with large outdoor tea parties held in celebration of Queen Elizabeth's Golden, Silver, and Sapphire Jubilees.

The grandest of all teas was the afternoon tea party hosted on the grounds of a great estate. These elaborate gatherings were held for everything from a sporting event—such as Downton Abbey's annual cricket match—to a charity fundraiser to an engagement party. In season 1, episode 7, of *Downton Abbey*, at a garden party in aid of a local hospital, we see footmen circulating among the guests carrying silver trays with stacks of finger sandwiches, while visible on the table in the white marquee is a selection of Victoria sponges, ginger cakes, loaf cakes, and other sweets.

PUBLIC TEAROOMS

Tea meetings and village tea parties were both part of tea's moving outside the confines of the domestic household and into public spaces, such as railway refreshment rooms, hotel restaurants, and, by the 1860s, commercial tearooms. The Aerated Bread Company opened the first A.B.C. tea shop in a railway station in 1864, and by the *Downton Abbey* era, in the 1920s, its empire numbered some 250 tearooms. Although some establishments were grand enough to welcome Lady Mary and Matthew on a visit to London in season 3, episode 8, many of them emulated an upper-class environment on a smaller scale to attract the lower classes, creating the very British feeling of afternoon tea as a moment to dress up like the gentry.

Because the tearoom was a predominantly female environment, it became a natural meeting place for members of the suffragette movement—a place where they could come together without men to plan their "Votes for Women" fight. Women were on the move, as Lady Edith's story idea for her magazine illustrates in season 6, episode 5: "Victorian babies grown up into modern women."

THE CORSET AND THE TEA GOWN

Up until the early twentieth century, women typically wore corsets for most of their lives, which gave their bodies the hyperfeminine, perfectly contoured shape fashionable at the time. The garments were magnificent, but they were also shackles, placing the wearer in a state of imprisonment that made it difficult to walk, breathe, or look natural.

Despite the extreme discomfort, not all women were against the corset. Indeed, contemporary publications often presented both positive and negative views on its wearing. Societal norms leveled pressure too, with many people believing that corsets were a moral requirement, a symbol of decency, and to be seen without one in public would be vulgar.

While Lady Mary and Lady Edith don't mind strapping on a corset, we see Lady Sybil complaining about the tightness of hers in season

2. When she asks Anna to loosen it, Edith is quick to say, "It's the start of a slippery slope." This scene is symbolic of Sybil's personal struggle with the place of a woman in society—especially an upper-class woman. The suffragette movement is in the headlines, and the First World War will see women trade housework for factory work or train as nurses. Suddenly, a woman doesn't just have to be pretty or have to be the cook and maid. She can have a job, earn money, and be independent. For Sybil, training and working as a nurse gives her the liberation she has long sought. Even Edith loosens her corset when she changes into trousers and last season's coat and volunteers to drive a tractor to help John Drake, one of the estate's tenant farmers.

There were only two occasions on which a lady was not required to wear a corset. The first would be in her bedroom, when she wore a robe, one reason why married women like Cora and later Lady Mary liked to take their breakfast in bed, delaying donning a confining corset and a dress. The second would be for afternoon tea, when wearing a tea gown was the fashion.

The tea gown, which became popular in the mid-nineteenth century, borrowed its form from a variety of sources. Early examples were modeled on the Japanese kimono and were typically loose-fitting, flowing gowns of silk or chiffon. Later designs often mixed distinct aspects of different fashion periods, such as the eighteenth-century *robe à la française*, with its unfitted back and front, Watteau pleats, and frilly hanging sleeves. Waistlines could be empire style or dropped quite low, as was the rage in the 1920s. Although designed for afternoon tea, by the *Downton Abbey* era, tea gowns were also commonly worn throughout the afternoon and evening, and Cora is sometimes seen in a tea gown around the house.

TEA AT DOWNTON ABBEY

In *Downton Abbey*, we often get a glimpse of tea being served both upstairs and downstairs. In season 6, episode 4, Violet and Lady Shackleton are having tea, an occasion Violet is using to gain support that will allow her to manipulate a situation to her benefit. The silver hot-water kettle stands on a warmer, so the duo can serve themselves hot tea without the need for servants in the room. Meanwhile, downstairs, the servants are also having tea. Daisy is serving everyone, pouring tea from a tall Brown Betty teapot. While downstairs, the tea break is a rare moment of free time during a busy day, upstairs, the young women of the household find the afternoon tea a safe environment in which to socialize in a more natural manner, away from the strict protocol of dinner.

TEA ETIQUETTE

Books on social etiquette and the management of the household were popular in the days of *Downton Abbey*, but anyone born into a family like the Crawleys would have been raised to know these rules by heart at a young age. To need a book on etiquette was to mark you an outsider.

According to Emily Post's *Etiquette in Society, in Business, in Politics, and at Home*, published in 1922, the following items should always be present on the tea tray: "a kettle which ought to be already boiling, with a spirit lamp under it, an empty tea-pot, a caddy of tea, a tea strainer and slop bowl, cream pitcher and sugar bowl, and, on a glass dish, lemon in slices. A pile of cups and saucers and a stack of little tea plates, all to match, with a napkin . . . folded on each plate."

For the food, Post writes, there would be either a tea table or a stand made of three small "shelves," each large enough for one "good-sized plate." The top plate, covered, "holds hot bread of some sort; . . . the second dish usually holds sandwiches, and the third, cake. Or perhaps all the dishes hold cake; little fancy cakes for instance, and pastries and slices of layer cakes." At Downton, we often see trays of small cakes, Victoria sponge, or fruitcake.

PREPARING THE TEA

- Bring a kettle filled with fresh cold water to a boil. If desired, pour a little boiling water into your teapot, swirl it around to warm the pot, and then pour it out.

- Add to the warmed teapot 1 teaspoon tea leaves per person plus 1 teaspoon for the pot.

- As soon as the water returns to a boil, pour it over the leaves in the pot.

- Allow the tea to steep for 2–5 minutes, depending on the preferred strength and the type of tea (black teas are typically steeped longer than white, green, or oolong teas). Set a pitcher filled with hot water on the tea tray so that guests who favor a weaker cup can dilute their serving.

SERVING THE TEA

The hostess traditionally both makes and pours the tea, a holdover from the days when women held the key to the tea caddy and therefore the power of the house. Each cup is poured—ideally through a tea strainer to capture loose leaves—and passed to a guest before the next cup is poured.

A guest then adds milk or a lemon slice to the cup. Milk is typically added to black tea, while lemon is traditionally paired with Lapsang Souchong. (In the past, before heat-resistant porcelain was commonplace, milk was added to the cup before the hot tea to guard against the china breaking.) Sugar is added last, and the tea is then stirred. Once the sugar has dissolved, the spoon is returned to the saucer.

The saucer always remains on the table when the cup is lifted to drink. The cup is grasped with the thumb and index finger meeting in the handle and the handle resting on the middle finger. Contrary to popular belief, the pinkie should never be held upright, which is considered rude. Finally, tea is sipped, not gulped, and the cup is returned to the saucer between sips.

BRITISH TEA CHARACTERISTICS

The first tea to arrive in England from China was green tea in the seventeenth century. The strong black tea that is now associated with English tea drinking is a legacy of British tea production in colonial India in the nineteenth century.

By the early nineteenth century, the British had developed such a taste for tea that they knew they had to expand their source beyond China. In the 1820s, the British East India Company, already established in colonial India, began extensive production in Assam using a local tea variety. The new enterprise flourished, delivering not only a steady supply of tea at a lower price to the home market but also a patriotic product for the empire.

In the late 1840s, the British East India Company, recognizing China's commanding expertise in the production and processing of tea, sent the Scottish botanist Robert Fortune to China to learn all he could about Chinese tea horticulture and manufacturing and to obtain the finest plants for replanting in India. Although Fortune arranged for thousands of tea plants to be shipped to India, all but a handful died. But the knowledge he had acquired and the experienced Chinese workers he brought to Assam to oversee processing paved the way not only for India to become one of the world's premier tea producers but also for tea to become part of everyday life across the British classes.

TYPES OF TEA

While traditional caffeinated teas are made from just two varieties of the *Camellia sinensis* tea plant, *C. sinensis* var. *sinensis* (Chinese tea) and *C. sinensis* var. *assamica* (Indian Assam tea), they yield a variety of different types of tea as a result of how the leaves are processed and blended.

GREEN TEA

Green tea originated in China and then spread to many other countries in Asia. It calls for very little processing apart from drying or steaming the leaves and then rolling them.

WHITE TEA

Once known as silvery tip pekoe because of its appearance, white tea is the lightest flavored of the five primary types. It is made from immature leaves and young buds covered with fine white hairs, both harvested by hand before they fully open and then minimally processed by quickly being dried.

BLACK TEA

Generally stronger in flavor than the other types, black tea undergoes four stages in processing: first the leaves are heavily withered, next they are tightly rolled, then they are allowed to oxidize completely under controlled temperature, and finally they are dried to stop the oxidation process.

OOLONG TEA

These leaves are allowed to oxidize partially and ferment under controlled temperature, after which they are curled and twisted to create their unique shape.

LAPSANG SOUCHONG

For this black tea, the rougher leaves of the tea plant are withered, rolled, oxidized, and then roasted over a pinewood fire, resulting in a distinctive smoky flavor.

BLENDED TEA

EARL GREY

Prized for its citrus notes, which it owes to the addition of bergamot (natural or synthetic), Earl Grey, the first mention of which appeared in the 1880s, was originally made from Keemun, a Chinese tea. To make it more appealing with milk, tea companies switched to a more boldly flavored black tea, which nowadays might be Ceylon, African, or Indian tea.

ENGLISH BREAKFAST

Despite the name, English breakfast tea, which dates to the late eighteenth century, first appeared in America, not Britain. It is a full-flavored tea made from Assam, Ceylon, and Kenya black teas, sometimes with the addition of milder Keemun.

IRISH BREAKFAST

A blended black tea made mostly from Assam, Irish breakfast is characterized by its red color and robust malty flavor that are perfect with the addition of milk.

Pastries, Buns
& Biscuits

ENGLISH CREAM SCONES

Scones have been essential to the British teatime tradition since the mid-nineteenth century, when, according to legend, the fashionable Duchess of Bedford ordered her servants to sneak the small cakes and hot tea into her room for an afternoon snack. In time, she began inviting her friends to join her for afternoon tea, and this homey ritual became a social trend. Queen Victoria, hearing of the new convention, soon began hosting fancy-dress tea parties. The tradition continued into the twentieth century, with Mrs. Patmore serving scones to Lord and Lady Grantham at her bed-and-breakfast in season 6 of *Downton Abbey*.

2 cups (250 g) flour, plus more for the work surface

1 tablespoon baking powder

2 teaspoons sugar, plus 1 tablespoon for sprinkling

1 teaspoon salt

½ cup (70 g) dried currants

¾ cup plus 2 tablespoons (200 ml) heavy cream

FOR THE TOPPING

1 egg white, lightly beaten with 1 teaspoon water

MAKES 10 SCONES

TEA ETIQUETTE

A scone should always be torn in two rather than cut with a knife, which would make the scone seem heavy.

Preheat the oven to 425°F (220°C). Have ready an ungreased sheet pan.

In a large bowl, whisk together the flour, baking powder, the 2 teaspoons sugar, and salt. Using a large spoon, stir in the currants and cream just until combined. Using your hands, gently gather the dough together, kneading it against the side of the bowl until it holds together in a rough ball.

Lightly flour a work surface and turn the dough out onto it. Roll out the dough about ¾ inch (2 cm) thick. Using a 3-inch (7.5-cm) round cutter, cut out rounds from the dough, pressing straight down and lifting straight up and spacing them as closely together as possible. Place the dough rounds at least 2 inches (5 cm) apart on the sheet pan. Gather up the dough scraps, knead briefly on the floured work surface, roll out the dough again, cut out more rounds, and add them to the pan.

Using a pastry brush, lightly brush the tops of the scones with the egg white mixture, then sprinkle evenly with the remaining sugar.

Bake the scones until golden, 10–12 minutes. Transfer to a wire rack to cool. Serve warm or at room temperature.

MADELEINES

These seashell-shaped French tea cakes were a customary addition to the afternoon tea tray at Downton and were kept in biscuit jars by the beds of Mary, Edith, and Sybil for late-night snacking. They were also a favorite of Matthew whose middle-class upbringing showed when, on his first visit to Downton, he loaded up his plate with the small, delicate cakelike madeleines.

4 tablespoons (60 g) unsalted butter, melted and cooled, plus room-temperature butter for the pan

½ cup (60 g) flour, plus more for the pan

2 eggs

⅓ cup (70 g) granulated sugar

¼ teaspoon salt

1 teaspoon pure vanilla extract

Confectioners' sugar, for dusting (optional)

MAKES 12 MADELEINES

Preheat the oven to 375°F (190°C). Using a pastry brush, coat the 12 molds of a madeleine pan with room-temperature butter, carefully coating each and every ridge. Dust the molds with flour, tilting the pan to coat evenly and then tapping out the excess.

In a bowl, using an electric mixer, beat together the eggs, granulated sugar, and salt on medium-high speed until light and fluffy, about 5 minutes. Beat in the vanilla. Turn off the mixer and sift the flour over the egg mixture. With the mixer on low speed, beat in the flour until fully incorporated. Turn off the mixer again and, using a rubber spatula, gently fold in half of the melted butter just until incorporated. Fold in the remaining melted butter just until blended.

Scoop a heaping tablespoonful of the batter into each prepared mold. Bake the madeleines, rotating the pan back to front halfway through baking, until the tops spring back when lightly pressed with a fingertip, 10–12 minutes. Remove the pan from the oven, immediately invert it onto a wire rack, and tap the pan on the rack to release the madeleines. If any of them stick, turn the pan upright, loosen their edges with a butter knife, and then invert and tap again. Let cool completely. If desired, lightly dust the tops with confectioners' sugar just before serving.

ENGLISH TOFFEE SHORTBREAD

The Scottish shortbread favored by Mary, Queen of Scots (see page 36), saw only minor changes until the twentieth century. One nineteenth-century variation that included ginger was favored by members of the Scottish Parliament, earning the snack the name Parliament Cakes. For this later innovation, a much-celebrated English candy, which even boasts its own holiday, National English Toffee Day, is mixed into the dough.

½ cup (115 g) cold unsalted butter, cut into cubes, plus room-temperature butter for the pan

1 cup (125 g) flour, plus more for pressing

⅓ cup (80 g) firmly packed light brown sugar

2½ tablespoons cornstarch

⅛ teaspoon kosher salt

¾ teaspoon pure vanilla extract

½ cup (60 g) coarsely chopped pecans

⅓ cup (60 g) finely chopped chocolate-covered English toffee

Granulated sugar, for sprinkling

MAKES 16 BARS

Preheat the oven to 350°F (180°C). Butter a 9-inch (23-cm) square or round cake pan.

In a food processor, combine the flour, brown sugar, cornstarch, and salt and process until blended, about 5 seconds. Scatter the cold butter over the flour mixture, add the vanilla, and, using rapid pulses, process until the mixture resembles fine meal. Add the pecans and process until finely chopped. Add the toffee and process just to incorporate.

Using lightly floured fingertips, press the dough into the prepared pan in an even layer. Sprinkle the surface evenly with granulated sugar.

Bake the shortbread just until it begins to color and the edges are golden, about 20 minutes. Let cool in the pan on a wire rack for 5 minutes, then cut into 16 bars or wedges, carefully transfer the bars to the rack, and let cool completely.

ROCK CAKES

The origin of these small, fun, craggy cakes is unknown, though they seem to date from at least the mid-eighteenth century. The dough comes together quickly with the help of a food processor, but it can also be made by hand, using your fingers to rub the flour mixture and butter together. Any type of dried fruit or combination of dried fruits can be used. Currants, golden raisins, cherries, apricots, and cranberries are good choices.

1¾ cups (220 g) flour, plus more for rolling

¼ cup (50 g) granulated sugar

1¾ teaspoons baking powder

¼ teaspoon salt

½ cup (115 g) cold unsalted butter, diced

½ cup (70 g) dried fruit of choice, in small pieces

1 egg, lightly whisked

2 tablespoons milk

Sanding sugar, for sprinkling (optional)

MAKES 12 SMALL CAKES

Preheat the oven to 375°F (190°C). Line two sheet pans with parchment paper or silicone mats.

In a food processor, combine the flour, granulated sugar, baking powder, and salt and process until blended, about 5 seconds. Scatter the butter over the flour mixture and process until the mixture resembles coarse meal, 8–10 seconds. Dump the mixture into a bowl and stir in the dried fruit. Pour the egg and milk over the top and, using a rubber spatula and one hand, mix and pinch until all the ingredients come together in a soft dough.

Divide the dough into 12 equal pieces (about 3 tablespoons each) and gently shape each piece into a mound. Arrange the mounds on the prepared pans, spacing them about 2½ inches (6 cm) apart. Sprinkle with the sanding sugar, if using.

Bake the cakes until golden brown and a toothpick inserted into the center of a cake comes out clean, 16–18 minutes. Let cool on the pans on wire racks for at least 5 minutes. Serve warm or at room temperature.

RECIPE NOTE

If you have not sprinkled the cakes with sanding sugar, they can be served warm from the oven lightly dusted with confectioners' sugar. They can also be smeared with butter and a smidgen of jam. They are best served the day they are baked and can be reheated in a low oven.

WELSH CAKES

The texture of these Welsh griddle cakes lies between that of a pancake and that of a biscuit or scone. This version is slightly sweeter than the traditional one and is delicious for both breakfast and teatime, especially on March 1, the feast day of Saint David, the patron saint of Wales. Serve them straight from the griddle as they are or sprinkled with confectioners' or cinnamon sugar.

1½ cups (190 g) flour, plus more for the work surface

¼ cup (50 g) sugar

1¼ teaspoons baking powder

¼ teaspoon salt

Pinch of ground nutmeg (optional)

½ cup (115 g) cold unsalted butter, diced, plus more for cooking

⅓ cup (45 g) dried currants

1 egg, lightly whisked

¼ cup (60 ml) milk

MAKES TEN 2¼-INCH
(5.5-CM) CAKES

In a food processor, combine the flour, sugar, baking powder, salt, and nutmeg (if using) and process until blended, about 5 seconds. Scatter the butter over the flour mixture and process until the mixture resembles coarse meal, 8–10 seconds. Transfer the mixture into a bowl and stir in the currants. Pour the egg and milk over the top and, using a rubber spatula and one hand, mix and pinch until all the ingredients come together in a soft, slightly sticky dough.

Scrape the dough onto a lightly floured work surface and press into a round about ½ inch (12 mm) thick, lightly flouring as necessary. Using a 2¼-inch (5.5-cm) round cutter, cut out as many rounds as possible. Gather together the scraps, press together into a round about ½ inch (12 mm) thick, and cut out more rounds. You should have a total of 10 rounds.

Heat a griddle or a cast-iron frying pan over medium-low heat. Drop a small piece of butter onto the hot surface and spread to coat the surface. Add as many cakes as will fit without crowding and cook until deep golden brown on the bottom, about 4 minutes. Reduce the heat if overbrowning. Flip the cakes and continue cooking until they are puffed, the underside is golden brown, and the sides no longer look wet, 4–5 minutes longer, adjusting the heat if necessary.

Transfer the cakes to a wire rack and let cool for 5 minutes before serving. Repeat with the remaining cakes, adding more butter to the griddle as needed. Serve warm.

PALMIERS

In Edwardian England, the ability to produce refined French pastry, such as the puff pastry used for *palmiers,* was an essential skill of cooks in the houses of the aristocracy. Although *palmier* is French for "palm tree," these flaky, crunchy cookies have taken on many names across the world, from pig's ears, elephant's ears, and *coeurs de France* to shoe soles, eyeglasses, and more.

2 tablespoons unsalted butter, melted

½ teaspoon pure vanilla extract

½ cup (100 g) granulated sugar

½ cup (60 g) confectioners' sugar

1 sheet frozen puff pastry, about ½ lb (225 g), thawed

1 egg, beaten with 1 tablespoon water

MAKES ABOUT 20 PALMIERS

TEA ETIQUETTE

The Crawleys use both their more elegant silver tea set as well as porcelain cups, saucers, and plates.

Preheat the oven to 375°F (190°C). Line two sheet pans with parchment paper.

In a small bowl, stir together the butter and vanilla. In another bowl, using a fork, stir together the granulated and confectioners' sugars. Measure out ½ cup (80 g) of the sugar mixture and set aside.

Sprinkle 3 tablespoons of the remaining sugar mixture onto a work surface. Place the puff pastry on top of the sugared surface. Sprinkle more of the sugar mixture on top of the pastry, spreading it evenly with your hands. Using a rolling pin and starting at the center of the pastry sheet, roll out the pastry into a 10-by-20-inch (25 x 50-cm) rectangle, always rolling from the center outward and rotating the sheet a quarter turn after every one or two passes with the pin. As you work, sprinkle a little more sugar mixture underneath and on top of the pastry as needed to prevent sticking.

Using a pastry brush, brush the butter mixture over the surface of the pastry. Sprinkle evenly with the reserved ½ cup (80 g) sugar mixture. Starting at one short end, fold a band of the pastry 2 inches (5 cm) wide over onto itself. Repeat this folding until you reach the center of the pastry. Fold the other end of the rectangle in the same way. Turn the folded side down and cut the rectangle crosswise into slices ½ inch (12 mm) thick. Place the slices on the prepared pans, spacing them 2 inches (5 cm) apart.

Bake the palmiers until golden, about 15 minutes. Let cool on the pans on wire racks for 5 minutes, then transfer them to the racks and let cool completely.

HOT CROSS BUNS

These sweet spiced buns, a hallmark of the Easter season, became popular in England in the seventeenth century, when rich yeast-risen doughs were in vogue. Perhaps even more commonly enjoyed for breakfast than for afternoon tea, hot cross buns were a staple of the Downton tables, both upstairs and downstairs, and were regularly seen cooling in Mrs. Patmore's kitchen.

3½–4 cups (440–500 g) flour, plus more for the work surface and bowl

¼ cup (50 g) superfine sugar

½ teaspoon ground nutmeg

½ teaspoon ground cinnamon

¼ teaspoon ground ginger

Generous pinch of salt

4 tablespoons (60 g) salted butter, plus more for the pan and for serving

1¼ cups (300 ml) milk

1 teaspoon active dry yeast

1 egg, lightly whisked

½ teaspoon grated lemon zest

½ teaspoon grated orange zest

½ cup (80 g) firmly packed dried currants

½ cup (90 g) diced mixed candied orange and lemon peel or golden raisins

MAKES 12 BUNS

In a large bowl, stir together 3½ cups (440 g) of the flour, the sugar, nutmeg, cinnamon, ginger, and salt, mixing well. Make a well in the center.

In a small saucepan over medium heat, combine the butter and milk and heat just until the butter melts. Remove from the heat and let cool to barely lukewarm (100°F/38°C), then add the yeast. Let stand until the yeast is foamy, about 5 minutes, then add the egg and citrus zests and stir until well mixed. Pour the yeast mixture into the well in the flour mixture and stir together with a wooden spoon until a shaggy dough forms.

Flour a work surface, turn the dough out onto it, and knead until smooth, soft, and elastic, about 20 minutes, adding only as much of the remaining ½ cup (60 g) flour, a little at a time, as needed to prevent sticking. Lightly flour a large bowl and transfer the dough to it. Cover the bowl with plastic wrap or a damp kitchen towel, set the bowl in a warm spot, and let the dough rise until doubled in size, about 1½ hours.

Lightly flour the work surface, turn the dough out onto it, and press the dough flat. Scatter the currants and candied peel evenly on top. Roll up the dough to enclose the fruits, then knead gently to distribute the fruits evenly. Cover with a bowl or a damp kitchen towel and let rest for 10 minutes.

Lightly butter a sheet pan. Divide the dough into 12 equal portions and shape each portion into a ball. As the balls are formed, place them, seam side down, on the prepared pan, spacing them evenly apart. Cover them loosely with a damp kitchen towel and leave them to rise in a warm spot until puffy, about 1 hour. After about 40 minutes of rising, preheat the oven to 375°F (190°C).

Using a very sharp knife, slash a cross in the top of each raised bun. Bake the buns until golden brown, 15–20 minutes. Transfer to a wire rack, let cool slightly, and eat hot, or let cool completely on the rack and serve at room temperature. Either way, offer butter at the table for slathering onto the buns.

GINGER BISCUITS

Also known as ginger nuts, these hard spiced biscuits (aka cookies) have been popular in Britain since the 1840s. Although similarly spiced, they are quite different from gingerbread, which is thicker and has a softer, breadlike texture. These no-frill sweets emerge from the oven quite soft but harden on cooling, making them perfect for dunking into a hot cup of afternoon tea.

2½ cups (310 g) flour

1½ teaspoons ground ginger

1 teaspoon baking soda

½ teaspoon ground cinnamon

¼ teaspoon ground cloves

¼ teaspoon salt

⅔ cup (160 ml) canola oil

1 cup (210 g) firmly packed light brown sugar

⅓ cup (115 g) dark molasses (black treacle)

1 whole egg, lightly whisked

¾ cup (130 g) chopped crystallized ginger

1 egg white

½ cup (115 g) coarse sugar

MAKES ABOUT 48 BISCUITS

Preheat the oven to 325°F (165°C). Line two sheet pans with parchment paper.

Combine the flour, ground ginger, baking soda, cinnamon, cloves, and salt in a sifter or fine-mesh sieve and set aside.

In a large bowl, using a wooden spoon, stir together the oil, brown sugar, and molasses until well combined. Add the whole egg and beat until blended. Sift the flour mixture into the oil mixture and stir until blended. Stir in the crystallized ginger.

In a small bowl, lightly whisk the egg white. Spread the coarse sugar in a shallow bowl.

With dampened hands, shape the dough into 1-inch (2.5-cm) balls. Brush each ball lightly with the egg white and then roll in the sugar to coat lightly. Place the dough balls about 1 inch (2.5 cm) apart on the prepared pans.

Bake the biscuits until the tops are set and crackled, 15–18 minutes. Let cool on the pans on wire racks for 5 minutes, then transfer to the racks and let cool completely, until firm.

CHOCOLATE FLORENTINES

Despite the seemingly eponymous name, not much is known about these elegant treats except that Florentines do not hail from Florence. Although their origin is a mystery, the thin, crisp, and delicate nature of the caramelized almond delicacies suggests both French pastry technique and a place on the afternoon tea menu.

FOR THE FLORENTINES
1 teaspoon grated orange zest

¼ cup (30 g) flour

5 tablespoons (70 g) unsalted butter, cut into pieces

¼ cup (60 ml) heavy cream

½ cup (100 g) sugar

2 tablespoons honey

¾ cup (70 g) sliced blanched almonds

FOR THE CHOCOLATE GLAZE

6 oz (170 g) semisweet chocolate, finely chopped

½ cup (115 g) unsalted butter

1 tablespoon light corn syrup

MAKES ABOUT
24 FLORENTINES

Preheat the oven to 325°F (165°C). Line two sheet pans with parchment paper.

To make the Florentines, in a small bowl, stir together the orange zest and flour until the zest is coated. Set aside.

In a saucepan over low heat, combine the butter, cream, sugar, and honey. Cook, stirring, until the butter melts and the sugar dissolves. Raise the heat to medium-high and bring to a boil, stirring constantly, then boil for 2 minutes. Remove from the heat and stir in the almonds, followed by the flour mixture. The batter will be thick. Drop the batter by 2-teaspoon scoops onto the prepared pans, spacing the Florentines about 3 inches (7.5 cm) apart. Flatten each Florentine with the back of the spoon.

Place one sheet pan in the oven and bake the cookies until they spread to about 3 inches (7.5 cm) in diameter, are bubbling vigorously, and are light brown at the edges, about 14 minutes. Let the Florentines cool on the pan on a wire rack for 10 minutes. Using a wide spatula, transfer them to the rack and let cool completely. Repeat with the second sheet pan.

To make the glaze, combine the chocolate, butter, and corn syrup in a heatproof bowl placed over (not touching) barely simmering water in a saucepan and heat, stirring often, until the chocolate and butter are melted, about 4 minutes. Remove from the heat and pour the glaze through a fine-mesh sieve into a heatproof bowl. Let cool to barely lukewarm before using.

Line a sheet pan with parchment paper. Dip half of each Florentine into the lukewarm glaze and place on the prepared pan. Let stand until the glaze sets, about 30 minutes.

SCOTTISH SHORTBREAD

Shortbread dates back to a hard, dry, sugar-dusted twelfth-century Scottish yeasted biscuit. In the mid-sixteenth century, Mary, Queen of Scots, encouraged her French pastry chefs to create a more refined version in which the yeast was traded out for butter and the dough was baked into a round, scallop-edged cake that was cut into wedges for serving. The last major change came in 1921, when British law mandated that any product labeled "shortbread" must derive at least 51 percent of its fat from butter, guaranteeing Downton residents a properly buttery treat.

1½ cups (190 g) flour, plus more for pressing

¼ teaspoon salt

1 cup (225 g) unsalted butter, at room temperature

¼ cup (30 g) confectioners' sugar

¼ cup (50 g) granulated sugar, plus 1 tablespoon for sprinkling

2 teaspoons pure vanilla extract

MAKES 12–16 BARS

Preheat the oven to 300°F (150°C). Have ready a 9-inch (23-cm) square baking pan.

Sift together the flour and salt into a bowl. In a large bowl, using an electric mixer, beat the butter on medium-high speed until fluffy and pale yellow, about 3 minutes. Add the confectioners' sugar and the ¼ cup (50 g) granulated sugar and beat until the mixture is well combined, then beat in the vanilla. On low speed, gradually add the flour mixture and beat just until blended.

Using lightly floured fingertips, press the dough into the baking pan in an even layer. Sprinkle the surface evenly with the remaining 1 tablespoon granulated sugar.

Bake the shortbread until the edges are golden, about 1 hour. Remove from the oven and, using a thin-bladed, sharp knife, immediately cut the shortbread into 12–16 bars. Using a fork, decorate each bar with a pattern of dots. Let cool in the pan on a wire rack for 30 minutes, then carefully transfer the bars to the rack and let cool completely.

PECAN TUILES

Tuiles, French for "tiles," are wafer-thin cookies arced to mimic the roof tiles on French country homes. The well-traveled members of the Crawley household would likely have been just as familiar with the delicate rounded sweets served in the best patisseries as they were with French architectural style. Pecans made their way to Europe from North America in the sixteenth century with returning Spanish explorers. Although tuiles are traditionally made with almonds, an innovative Parisian pastry chef would have hit upon the idea of using the New World nut in their place.

½ cup (60 g) pecans, plus
⅓ cup (40 g) finely chopped

½ cup (100 g) sugar

¼ cup (30 g) flour

5 tablespoons (70 g) unsalted butter, melted and cooled, plus room-temperature butter for the pan

2 egg whites, lightly whisked

½ teaspoon pure vanilla extract

MAKES 24 TUILES

RECIPE NOTE

To achieve the classic tuile shape, the wafer must be shaped on a curved surface while still hot.

Preheat the oven to 350°F (180°C). Butter a large sheet pan.

In a food processor, combine the ½ cup (60 g) pecans and the sugar and process until finely ground. Transfer to a bowl. Stir in the flour, followed by the butter, egg whites, and vanilla, and mix well.

Working in batches, spoon the batter by heaping teaspoonfuls onto the prepared pan, spacing the mounds at least 3 inches (7.5 cm) apart. Using an icing spatula or a dinner knife, spread each mound into a round 2½ inches (6 cm) in diameter. Sprinkle each round with a generous ½ teaspoon of the chopped pecans.

Bake the cookies until the edges are darkly golden and the centers are lightly golden, about 9 minutes. Using a thin, flexible metal spatula and working quickly, lift each tuile from the sheet pan and drape it over a rolling pin. Let cool until firm, about 1 minute, then carefully transfer to a wire rack to cool completely. If the tuiles cool too much on the pan and become brittle, return the pan to the oven briefly to soften them. Repeat with the remaining batter and chopped pecans, always allowing the pan to cool before buttering it for the next batch.

CANELÉS

A specialty of Bordeaux, *canelés* are believed to have first been baked by nuns in the city's Convent of the Annonciades about three hundred years ago. The small cakes—rich and moist on the inside, dark brown on the outside—largely disappeared after the French Revolution due to the forced closure of the pastry guild devoted to their production. They resurfaced in French pastry shops in the early twentieth century, however, and soon became an elegant teatime treat in neighboring Britain.

2¼ cups (525 ml) milk

1 vanilla bean, split lengthwise

2 whole eggs

2 egg yolks

1¼ cups (250 g) sugar

1 cup (125 g) plus 2 tablespoons flour

4 tablespoons (60 g) unsalted butter, melted, plus 2 tablespoons, melted, for the molds

1 tablespoon light rum

MAKES 15 – 18 PASTRIES

Pour the milk into a saucepan. Using the tip of a knife, scrape the seeds from the vanilla bean into the milk, then add the pod halves. Place over medium-high heat and heat until small bubbles appear along the edges of the pan, about 5 minutes. Remove from the heat and let cool to warm.

In a small bowl, whisk the whole eggs until blended. In another small bowl, whisk the egg yolks until blended. In a large bowl, whisk together the sugar and flour. Make a well in the center of the flour mixture, add the whole eggs and then the egg yolks to the well, and whisk to create a thick paste. Remove the vanilla pod from the milk and discard. Add the warm milk, melted butter, and rum to the egg mixture and whisk until well blended. Cover the bowl with plastic wrap and refrigerate for at least 1 hour or up to 2 hours.

Preheat the oven to 350°F (180°C). Using a pastry brush, brush canelé molds with some of the remaining 2 tablespoons melted butter and refrigerate for 15 minutes. (If you do not have canelé molds, butter 12 standard muffin cups using all the butter.)

Stir the batter well, then fill each chilled mold (or muffin cup) almost to the rim. Place the molds on a sheet pan. Bake the canelés until they are dark brown and puffed on the edges with a slight depression in the center, about 1 hour; do not open the oven door during baking. Remove the canelés from the oven and unmold them onto a wire rack while they are still hot. Continue buttering, chilling, and filling the molds and baking the canelés until all of the batter has been used, always refrigerating the batter between batches.

Serve the canelés warm or at room temperature.

CHELSEA BUNS

Introduced in the early 1700s at the Chelsea Bun House in South West London, this currant bun, made famous by proprietor Richard Hand—aka Captain Bun—became the must-have treat for that era and beyond. The royal family was known to be such avid fans of the square, fruit-filled yeasted bun that the bakery was nicknamed the Royal Bun House.

FOR THE DOUGH

3 cups (375 g) flour

3 tablespoons sugar

2 teaspoons quick-rise yeast

1 teaspoon salt

1 cup (240 ml) whole milk, warmed (115°–125°F/45°–52°C)

4 tablespoons (60 g) unsalted butter, melted

Nonstick cooking spray or neutral oil, for the bowl

FOR THE FILLING

3 tablespoons sugar

2 teaspoons mixed spice or pumpkin pie spice

3 tablespoons unsalted butter, melted

1 cup (140 g) dried currants

FOR THE GLAZE

¼ cup (50 g) granulated sugar

2 tablespoons very hot tap water

MAKES 9 BUNS

To make the dough, in the bowl of a stand mixer, whisk together the flour, sugar, yeast, and salt, then fit the mixer with the dough hook. Turn the mixer on medium-low speed, pour the milk and butter into the flour mixture, and beat until the flour is completely incorporated. Increase the speed to medium and beat until the dough is shiny and pulls away from the bottom of the bowl, 8–10 minutes. If the dough climbs up the hook, stop the mixer and scrape down the dough into the bowl.

Transfer the dough to a work surface, knead once or twice until it no longer sticks to the surface, and shape into a ball. Lightly grease the sides of the mixer bowl, then put the dough back into the bowl. Cover the bowl with a plate or plastic wrap, place in a warm spot, and let the dough rise until doubled in size, about 1 hour.

Lightly grease a 9-inch (23-cm) square baking pan with 2-inch (5-cm) sides. (For the best results, use a straight-sided pan.) To make the filling, in a small bowl, whisk together the sugar and mixed spice until well blended. Set aside along with the butter and currants.

Recipe continues on the following page

VIOLET: *Ah. Just the ticket. Nanny always said sweet tea was the thing for frayed nerves. Though why it has to be sweet I couldn't tell you.*

~ SEASON 1, EPISODE 3

Continued

To shape and fill the buns, scrape the dough out onto a work surface (no flour needed) and press down on it to deflate it. Using your hands or a rolling pin, shape the dough into a 9 x 18-inch (23 x 46-cm) rectangle, with a short side facing you. Pour the melted butter into the center of the dough rectangle and, using an offset spatula, spread it evenly to the edges. Sprinkle the sugar mixture evenly over the butter. Scatter the currants on top and press gently into the dough.

Roll up the dough Swiss roll–style and pinch to seal the seam. Position the roll, seam side down, on the work surface and reshape it into a log about 9 inches (23 cm) long. Using a serrated knife, trim off the ends, then cut the log into 9 slices each 1 inch (2.5 cm) thick. Arrange the slices, with a cut side down, in three rows in the prepared pan.

Loosely but completely cover the baking pan with storage wrap and place in a warm spot. Let the buns rise until they are puffed, fill the pan, and have taken on a square appearance, about 1 hour. About 40 minutes into the rising, preheat the oven to 350°F (180°C).

Meanwhile, make the glaze. In a small bowl, stir together the sugar and water until the sugar dissolves. Set aside.

Bake the buns until they are puffed and deep golden brown, 42–45 minutes. Transfer the pan to a wire rack, spoon the glaze evenly over the buns, and let the buns cool for about 15 minutes. Serve warm.

PRINCE OF WALES BISCUITS

The original version of this confection, popular in the Regency period of the early 1800s, was a sturdy, unsweetened biscuit (aka cookie) stamped with the traditional feather emblem of the Prince. Made by commercial bakers, it was served after dinner for dunking into sweet wine. This newer, softer version is lightly sweetened and makes a delicious addition to the teatime plate. The Prince would give you permission to forgo his feathers and use any decorative stamp you like.

2⅓ cups (300 g) flour, plus more for dipping

½ teaspoon salt

¾ cup (170 g) cold unsalted butter, diced

½ cup (100 g) sugar

1 egg

1 teaspoon pure vanilla extract

MAKES ABOUT 17 BISCUITS

TEA ETIQUETTE

These biscuits have a low percentage of sugar, so don't expect browning. If you want a slightly sweeter cookie, increase the sugar amount to ⅔ cup (140 g).

Preheat the oven to 350°F (180°C). Line three sheet pans with parchment paper.

In a medium bowl, whisk together the flour and salt. In a large bowl, using an electric mixer, beat the butter on medium speed until smooth, about 1 minute. Add the sugar, increase the speed to medium-high, and beat until fluffy and lighter in color, 2–3 minutes. Add the egg and vanilla and beat until fully incorporated. On medium-low speed, add the flour mixture and beat just until blended.

Put a few spoonfuls of flour in a small, shallow bowl to use for dipping. Using your hands, shape the dough into 1½-inch (4-cm) balls each weighing about 1¼ oz (35 g)—about the size of a golf ball—and set aside on a work surface. Working with 6 dough balls at a time, dip half of each ball into the flour to coat the upper half lightly and arrange the balls, flour side up and about 3 inches (7.5 cm) apart, on a prepared pan. Lightly flour a 3-inch (7.5-cm) cookie stamp and gently but firmly flatten the dough ball until the dough reaches the edges of the stamp (any excess can be trimmed away with the tip of a knife). Carefully lift off the stamp. Repeat the flouring and pressing with the remaining dough balls, arranging them on the remaining two sheet pans.

Bake one sheet pan at a time (slide the remaining pans into the refrigerator if the kitchen is warm) until the biscuits are pale golden brown around the edges (the bottoms will be more golden brown than the edges), 15–17 minutes. Let the biscuits cool on the pan on a wire rack for 10 minutes, then serve. The biscuits are best when served the same day.

RASPBERRY MERINGUES

French chef François Massialot, father of the crème brûlée, published the first meringue recipe in *Nouveau cuisinier royal et bourgeois*, his multivolume cookbook that began appearing in 1691. Large, featherlight meringue shells, usually filled with raspberries and topped with cream, are a favorite sweet course on the Downton dining table. Piping meringue into small nests yields an ideal adaptation for afternoon tea.

FOR THE MERINGUE

2 egg whites

1 teaspoon fresh lemon juice

½ cup plus 1 tablespoon (115 g) superfine sugar

FOR THE FOOL

½ lb (225 g) raspberries

½ cup plus 2 tablespoons (150 ml) heavy cream

¼ cup (50 g) superfine sugar

Confectioners' sugar, if needed

Raspberries, for serving

MAKES 6 MERINGUES

To make the meringue, preheat the oven to 200°F (95°C). Line a sheet pan with parchment paper.

In a bowl, using a whisk or a handheld mixer on medium speed, beat together the egg whites and lemon juice until soft peaks form, increasing the mixer speed to medium-high once the whites are foamy and begin to thicken. While beating constantly, add the superfine sugar, a little at a time, and beat until stiff peaks form.

Fit a piping bag with a large star tip, spoon the whipped egg whites into the bag, and secure closed. Pipe 6 meringue nests each 2–3 inches (5–7.5 cm) in diameter—first outlining them, then filling the centers, and finally building up the sides—and some small stars for garnish on the prepared pan.

Bake the meringues for 2–2½ hours. They should be crisp to the touch and lift off the parchment easily. Let cool completely.

To make the fool, in a food processor or blender, purée the raspberries, then pass the purée through a fine-mesh sieve to remove the seeds. Alternatively, use a food mill to purée the berries, which will extract the seeds as it purées. (Removing the seeds is optional but would have been done in houses like Downton.)

In a bowl, using a whisk or a handheld mixer on medium speed, whip together the cream and superfine sugar until soft peaks form. Using a rubber spatula, gently fold the raspberry purée into the whipped cream just until no white streaks remain.

MRS. PATMORE: *Now, what else can I give you? Another cup of tea, why not?*

MASON: *I don't mind if I do.*

~ SEASON 6, EPISODE 5

Taste and adjust with confectioners' sugar if you prefer it sweeter. The fool should be fairly tart, however, to contrast with the meringue.

Just before serving, fill the meringue nests with the fool and top with the small star meringues. Serve with a small cluster of raspberries alongside.

CRUMPETS

Originally a thin cake cooked on a hot griddle, the crumpet, a regular feature on both the afternoon tea tray and morning breakfast table, likely owes its name and its ancestry to the dry, dense fourteenth-century crompid cake. Elizabeth Raffald introduced the soft, spongy, crater-topped modern crumpet in her 1769 book *The Experienced English Housekeeper,* dubbing it a pikelet, a term still in use for the crumpet in parts of northern England.

3¼ cups (405 g) flour

4 teaspoons salt

½ teaspoon baking soda

2 cups (480 ml) milk, 1 cup (240 ml) heated to 115°F (46°C) and 1 cup (240 ml) at room temperature

2 tablespoons sugar

1 teaspoon active dry yeast

Unsalted butter, for the molds, pan, and serving

Jam, for serving

MAKES 12 CRUMPETS

In a medium bowl, whisk together the flour, salt, and baking soda. In a large bowl, if using a handheld mixer, or in the bowl of a stand mixer, combine the heated milk, sugar, and yeast and let stand until foamy, about 10 minutes. On low speed, slowly add the flour mixture and then the room-temperature milk, beating until a smooth, thick batter forms. Cover the bowl loosely with plastic wrap and set in a warm place until the batter expands and becomes bubbly, about 1 hour.

Heat a 12-inch (30-cm) cast-iron frying pan over medium heat. While the pan is heating, butter as many 4-inch (10-cm) ring molds as will fit comfortably in the pan. When the pan is hot, lightly grease it with butter, then place the prepared molds in the pan. Fill each ring with about ⅓ cup (80 ml) batter and cook until bubbles appear on the surface, about 6 minutes. Carefully remove the rings and flip the crumpets over. Cook until the crumpets are golden on the second side and cooked through, about 5 minutes. Transfer to a plate and keep warm.

Repeat with the remaining batter, buttering the ring molds each time. Serve hot with butter and jam.

ÉCLAIRS

Éclairs appear at Downton at the end of season 6 in one of the more eventful episodes. As Mary worries about accepting Henry Talbot, Edith's latest love affair seems to have ended in disaster, Thomas is recovering from his suicide attempt, and Mrs. Patmore's Bed and Breakfast is embroiled in scandal. Amid all this, it's something of a relief to see Daisy busy filling choux pastry with custard. Éclairs and their cousins, profiteroles, originated at the turn of the nineteenth century but didn't become popular for decades.

FOR THE PASTRY CREAM

1½ cups (350 ml) milk

1 vanilla bean, split lengthwise

4 egg yolks

½ cup (100 g) sugar

2 tablespoons cornstarch

2 tablespoons unsalted butter

FOR THE CHOUX PASTRY

½ cup (120 ml) milk

½ cup (120 ml) water

6 tablespoons (90 g) unsalted butter, cut into ½-inch (12-mm) pieces

¼ teaspoon salt

1 cup (125 g) flour

4 eggs

FOR THE GANACHE

4 oz (115 g) bittersweet or semisweet chocolate, coarsely chopped

4 tablespoons (60g) unsalted butter, cut into ½-inch (12-mm) pieces

¼ cup (60 ml) milk or freshly brewed strong coffee

MAKES 10 PASTRIES

To make the pastry cream, pour the milk into a saucepan. Using the tip of a knife, scrape the seeds from the vanilla bean into the milk, then add the pod halves. Place over medium heat and heat until small bubbles appear along the edges of the pan. Remove from the heat and remove the vanilla pod.

In a bowl, whisk together the egg yolks, sugar, and cornstarch until smooth. While whisking constantly, slowly add the hot milk to the egg yolk mixture until blended. Pour the blended mixture back into the saucepan and place over medium-low heat. Cook, whisking constantly, until the mixture comes to a boil and thickens, about 3 minutes. Continue cooking, whisking constantly, for 1 minute longer. Pour through a fine-mesh sieve into a clean bowl. Add the butter and stir until melted and the mixture is smooth. Cover the bowl with storage wrap, pressing it directly onto the surface of the cream to prevent a skin from forming, then poke a few holes in the plastic with the tip of a knife to allow steam to escape. Refrigerate until well chilled, at least 2 hours or up to 2 days.

To make the choux pastry, combine the milk, water, butter, and salt in a saucepan over medium-high heat and bring to a full boil. When the butter melts, remove the pan from the heat, add the flour all at once, and stir vigorously with a wooden spoon until blended.

Return the pan to medium heat and continue stirring until the mixture leaves the sides of the pan and forms a ball. Remove from the heat and let cool for 3–4 minutes, or until cooled to 140°F (60°C) on an instant-read thermometer.

Recipe continues on the following page

Continued

Meanwhile, in a small bowl, whisk 1 egg. When the batter has cooled, pour the egg into the batter and beat with the spoon until incorporated. Add the remaining 3 eggs, one at a time, whisking each one first in the small bowl and then mixing it into the batter. After each egg is added, the mixture will separate and appear shiny, but it will return to a smooth paste with vigorous beating. Let the paste cool for about 10 minutes before shaping.

Position two racks evenly spaced in the center of the oven and preheat the oven to 425°F (220°C). Line two sheet pans with parchment paper or aluminum foil.

To shape the éclair shells, fit a piping bag with a ¾-inch (2-cm) plain tip, spoon the dough into the bag, and secure closed. Pipe out logs 4 inches (10 cm) long and 1 inch (2.5 cm) wide onto the prepared pans, spacing the logs at least 2 inches (5 cm) apart to allow for expansion.

Bake the logs for 15 minutes, then reduce the heat to 375°F (190°C) and continue baking until golden brown, 15–20 minutes longer. Remove from the oven and immediately prick the side of each log with the tip of a sharp knife. Return the pans to the oven, leave the oven door ajar, and allow the pastries to dry out for 10–15 minutes. Remove from the oven once again and let the pastries cool completely on the pans on wire racks before filling.

To make the ganache, combine the chocolate and butter in a heatproof bowl. In a small saucepan over medium-high heat, bring the milk to a boil. Remove the milk from the heat and immediately pour it over the chocolate and butter, then whisk until the chocolate and butter melt and are smooth. Transfer the ganache to a wide bowl.

Using a sharp serrated knife, cut each log in half lengthwise. One at a time, hold the top half of each pastry upside down and dip the top surface into the ganache. Turn the dipped half right side up, place on a wire rack, and let stand until set, about 15 minutes.

Fit a piping bag with a ¾-inch (2-cm) plain or star tip, spoon the pastry cream into the bag, and secure closed. Pipe the cream into the bottom half of each log. Set the ganache-topped half on top of the cream. Serve at once, or refrigerate for up to 2 hours before serving.

RASPBERRY MACARONS

John Murrell's *A Daily Exercise for Ladies and Gentlewomen,* published in London in 1617, includes a recipe for the French *macaron,* a small, sweet confection made from Jordan almonds, rose water, sugar, egg whites, and ambergris. But more than two centuries would pass before French bakers began sandwiching a filling between two meringue-based macarons, creating the *macaron parisien* popular today.

1⅓ cups (145 g) superfine almond flour

2 cups (225 g) confectioners' sugar

3 large egg whites

½ teaspoon pure vanilla extract

½ teaspoon pure almond extract

Pinch of salt

3 drops rose-pink gel paste food coloring, plus more if needed

½ cup (140 g) seedless raspberry jam

MAKES ABOUT 25 MACARONS

Line two sheet pans with parchment paper. Combine the almond flour and 1 cup (115 g) of the confectioners' sugar in a sifter or fine-mesh sieve and reserve.

In a large bowl, using an electric mixer, beat together the egg whites, vanilla and almond extracts, and salt on medium speed until soft peaks form, about 3 minutes. Increase the speed to high and gradually beat in the remaining 1 cup (110 g) confectioners' sugar, beating until stiff peaks form. Add the food coloring and beat until fully incorporated, adding more if needed to achieve the desired shade of pink.

Sift about one-fourth of the almond-sugar mixture over the beaten whites. Using a rubber spatula, fold it in until blended. Repeat with the remaining almond-sugar mixture in three equal batches, folding until incorporated and the batter flows like lava.

Fit a piping bag with a ⅜-inch (1-cm) plain tip, spoon the batter into the bag, and secure closed. Holding the piping bag with the tip about ½ inch (12 mm) above a prepared sheet pan, pipe about 25 mounds, each 1½–1¾ inches (4–4.5 cm) in diameter, onto each sheet pan, spacing the mounds about 1 inch (2.5 cm) apart. Make the mounds as smooth as possible, moving the bag off to one side after each mound is piped. Tap each sheet firmly against the work surface two or three times to release any air bubbles, then let stand at room temperature for 30–45 minutes.

Position a rack in the lower third of the oven and preheat the oven to 325°F (165°C). Bake one sheet pan at a time, rotating the pan back to front halfway through baking, until the macarons have risen

and just set but not browned, 10–11 minutes. The bottom of each
macaron should be dry and firm to the touch. Transfer the macarons
to a wire rack and let cool completely.

Turn half of the macarons bottom side up on a work surface and
spoon about ½ teaspoon jam onto each bottom. Top them with
the remaining macarons, bottom side down. Arrange the macarons
in a single layer on a sheet pan, cover with rstorage wrap, and
refrigerate for at least 1 day or up to 3 days before serving. Serve
chilled or at cool room temperature.

Cakes, Tarts
& Puddings

BATTENBERG CAKE

Also known as a domino cake or church window cake, this almond-flavored checkerboard-style confection was named in honor of the 1884 marriage of Queen Victoria's granddaughter Victoria to Prince Louis of Battenberg. Because of anti-German sentiment in Britain during World War I, the Prince gave up his German name and dynastic titles in 1917 and took an English name, Mountbatten (the surname of the current Prince Philip of England, his grandson).

FOR THE CAKE

¾ cup (170 g) unsalted butter, at room temperature, plus more for the pan and foil

1⅓ cups (170 g) all-purpose flour, plus more for the pan and foil

⅓ cup (40 g) almond flour

1 teaspoon baking powder

½ teaspoon salt

1 cup (200 g) granulated sugar

3 eggs, at room temperature

¾ teaspoon pure vanilla extract

½ teaspoon pure almond extract

¼ cup (60 ml) milk

1–3 drops red or pink food coloring

FOR ASSEMBLY

⅓ cup (105 g) apricot jam

Confectioners' sugar, for dusting

1 tube (7 oz/198 g) marzipan (preferably white)

SERVES 8–10

To make the cake, preheat the oven to 325°F (165°C). Lightly butter the bottom and sides of an 8-inch (20-cm) square cake pan with 2-inch (5-cm) sides. Cut an 8 x 12-inch (20 x 30-cm) rectangle of aluminum foil. Fold it in half crosswise to create an 8 x 6-inch (20 x 15-cm) rectangle. Fold both ends toward the centerfold to make an edge 2 inches (5 cm) high from the center. Crease the edges of the folds (top and both bottom) firmly and unfold the sides. It will look like an upside-down T. Arrange the foil sheet in the greased pan (the center fold will divide the pan into two separate sections each 8 by 4 inches/20 by 10 cm). Lightly butter the foil and flour the sides of the pan and the foil.

In a bowl, whisk together the all-purpose flour, almond flour, baking powder, and salt. In a large bowl, using an electric mixer, beat the butter on medium speed until smooth, about 1 minute. Increase the speed to medium-high, add the granulated sugar, and beat until fluffy and lighter in color, 2–3 minutes. Add the eggs, one at a time, beating well after each addition and adding the vanilla and almond extracts along with the final egg. On low speed, add about half of the flour mixture and mix just until blended, then add the milk and again mix until blended. Add the remaining flour and mix just until blended.

Divide the batter in half (about 14 oz/400 g each). Scrape half of the batter into one side of the divided pan and spread evenly. Add 1 drop of the food coloring to the remaining batter and fold until evenly colored, adding more food coloring as needed to achieve the pink intensity desired. Scrape the pink batter into the other side of the pan and spread evenly.

Recipe continues on the following page

Bake the cakes until a toothpick inserted into the center of each side comes out clean, 32–34 minutes. Let cool in the pan on a wire rack for about 15 minutes. Run a thin-bladed knife around the inside of the pan to loosen the cake sides. Invert a rack on top of the pan and, using pot holders, grip the pan and the rack and invert together. Gently lift off the pan, peel away the foil, and let the cakes cool completely.

To assemble the cake, in a small saucepan, warm the jam over low heat until fluid, then pass it through a fine-mesh sieve set over a small bowl, pressing on the solids.

Place a cake, top side up, on a work surface. Using a serrated knife, cut away the domed top to level the cake. Trim the four sides to make them even, then measure the height of the cake (about 1¼ inches/3 cm). Using a ruler, cut the layer lengthwise into 2 strips that are the same width as the height of the cake. You should now have 2 strips of equal height and width. Repeat with the remaining cake, leveling the top and cutting into 2 strips. You should now have 4 strips of equal height and width. Trim all 4 strips to equal length (about 7 inches/18 cm long).

Lightly dust a work surface with confectioners' sugar. Place the marzipan on the dusted surface and, using a rolling pin, roll out the marzipan into an 8 x 11½-inch (20 x 29-cm) rectangle. Lightly dust with more confectioners' sugar if the marzipan is sticky. Trim off the edges to make a 7 x 10½-inch (18 x 26.5-cm) rectangle.

Arrange the marzipan with a long side facing you. Using an offset spatula, spread a thin layer of the jam crosswise down the center 5 inches (13 cm) of the marzipan. Arrange a pink cake strip on the left side on top of the jam, pressing gently. Spread a thin layer of the jam over the inside edge of the cake strip and arrange a plain cake strip next to it. Gently press the strips together. Spread a thin layer of jam over the tops of the strips and repeat with the remaining strips and jam, stacking the cake strips in reverse order like a checkerboard.

Spread a thin coating of jam over the top and sides of the stacked strips. Lift one side of the marzipan over the cake, pressing gently to adhere to the side. Using a fingertip, brush a little water over the marzipan edge on the top of the cake. Repeat with the other side of the marzipan, again pressing gently against the side of the cake and then pressing on the overlapping portion of the marzipan to seal the edges. Turn the cake over so the seam is on the bottom and then wrap in storage wrap. Refrigerate for at least 1 hour or up to 3 days.

Serve chilled or at room temperature, cut into slices.

ORANGE BUTTER CAKES

Sweet oranges were largely unknown in Europe until the fifteenth and sixteenth centuries, when Italian and Portuguese merchants encouraged their cultivation in the Mediterranean area. But they would not be widely available in the cold climes of northern Europe until the nineteenth century, when newly established rail systems began transporting fresh foods. British bakers, who had long been fond of uniting plain cake with fresh fruit, might well have turned out these little teatime cakes, each topped with a thin orange slice, to celebrate this latest addition to their larder.

6 tablespoons (90 g) unsalted butter, melted and cooled, plus ½ cup (115 g) and more for the ramekins, at room temperature

2 oranges

¾ cup (155 g) firmly packed light brown sugar

1 cup (125 g) flour

1 teaspoon baking powder

½ teaspoon baking soda

¼ teaspoon salt

½ cup (100 g) granulated sugar

2 eggs, at room temperature

¼ cup (60 ml) heavy cream, at room temperature

1 teaspoon pure vanilla extract

MAKES 6 SMALL CAKES

Preheat the oven to 350°F (180°C). Lightly butter six 1-cup (240-ml) ramekins or custard cups.

Grate the zest of 1 orange; reserve the fruit for another use. Cut the second orange crosswise into 6 very thin slices; you may not need the whole orange.

Sprinkle 2 tablespoons of the brown sugar onto the bottom of each prepared ramekin. Pour 1 tablespoon of the melted butter into each ramekin, evenly covering the sugar. Place 1 orange slice in each ramekin. Place the ramekins on a sheet pan.

Sift together the flour, baking powder, baking soda, and salt into a small bowl. In a large bowl, using an electric mixer, beat the remaining ½ cup (115 g) butter on medium speed until smooth, about 1 minute. Increase the speed to medium-high, add the granulated sugar and orange zest, and beat until fluffy and lighter in color, 3–5 minutes. Add the eggs, one at a time, beating well after each addition. Using a rubber spatula, fold in the flour mixture until well blended. Add the cream and vanilla and stir until thoroughly incorporated.

Divide the batter evenly among the ramekins, spooning it over the orange slices. Bake the cakes until the tops are golden and a toothpick inserted into the center of a cake comes out clean, about 35 minutes. Let the ramekins cool on the pan on a wire rack for 10 minutes.

Recipe continues on the following page

Continued

Run a thin-bladed knife around the edge of each ramekin to loosen the cake sides. Working with 1 cake at a time, invert a small dessert plate over the ramekin, then invert the ramekin and plate together in a single quick motion. Lightly tap the bottom of the ramekin with the knife handle to loosen the cake, then lift off the ramekin. If an orange slice sticks to a ramekin, loosen it with the knife tip and replace it on the cake. Serve the cakes warm or at room temperature.

GINGER BUTTER CAKE

Believed to have originated in Southeast Asia, ginger was a highly coveted import to the Roman Empire. It was already widely available in England in Anglo-Saxon times, and by the late Middle Ages, it was almost as common as pepper and was added to all manner of dishes. Since the eighteenth century, its culinary use has been primarily limited to baked goods, such as this simple teatime cake.

¾ cup (170 g) unsalted butter, at room temperature, plus more for the pan

2 cups (250 g) cake flour, plus more for the pan

¾ cup (130 g) chopped crystallized ginger, minced

⅓ cup (80 ml) Grand Marnier or other orange liqueur

2 teaspoons baking powder

2 teaspoons ground ginger

1¼ cups (140 g) confectioners' sugar, sifted, plus more for dusting

1 tablespoon light corn syrup

4 eggs

Grated zest of 1 orange

3-inch (7.5-cm) piece fresh ginger, peeled and grated

½ teaspoon pure almond extract

½ cup (120 ml) milk

SERVES 8

Preheat the oven to 350°F (180°C). Butter the bottom and sides of a 9 x 5 x 3-inch (23 x 13 x 7.5-cm) loaf pan, then dust with flour, tapping out the excess.

In a small bowl, combine the crystallized ginger and Grand Marnier and let stand for 10 minutes. Sift together the flour, baking powder, and ground ginger into a bowl.

In a large bowl, using an electric mixer, beat the butter on medium speed until smooth, about 1 minute. Increase the speed to medium-high, add the sifted confectioners' sugar and corn syrup, and beat until fluffy and lighter in color, 4–5 minutes. Add the eggs, one at a time, beating well after each addition. Add the orange zest, fresh ginger, and almond extract and beat until blended.

Using a rubber spatula, gently fold in one-third of the flour mixture until almost fully incorporated. Fold in half of the milk, followed by half of the remaining flour mixture and then the remaining milk. Add the remaining flour mixture and the liqueur-soaked crystallized ginger and fold in just until the batter is smooth and the flour mixture is fully incorporated. Do not overmix or the cake will be tough.

Transfer the batter to the prepared pan, spread evenly, and smooth the top. Bake the cake until a toothpick inserted into the center comes out clean, 50–60 minutes. Let cool in the pan on a wire rack for at least 5 minutes, then turn the cake out onto the rack and turn the cake right side up. Lightly dust the top with confectioners' sugar just before serving. Serve warm or at room temperature.

MINI VICTORIA SPONGE CAKES

Also known as a Victoria sandwich, the Queen's actual teatime sponge cake would have been sandwiched with only a thick layer of raspberry jam and topped with a sprinkle of sugar. The earliest recipe for this buttery vanilla-infused cake appeared in *Mrs. Beeton's Household Management*, published in London in 1861. The addition of a layer of whipped cream or buttercream is a recent innovation but one the Grantham family would likely have enjoyed.

FOR THE CAKE

1 cup (225 g) unsalted butter, at room temperature, plus more for the ramekins

2 cups (250 g) flour, plus more for the ramekins

1½ teaspoons baking powder

½ teaspoon salt

1 cup (200 g) granulated sugar

4 large eggs, at room temperature

2 teaspoons pure vanilla extract

FOR THE FILLING

1¼ cups (300 ml) heavy cream

2 tablespoons confectioners' sugar

⅔ cup (210 g) strawberry or raspberry jam

Confectioners' sugar, for dusting

MAKES 12 SMALL CAKES

To make the cake, put an 11 x 17-inch (29 x 43-cm) sheet pan in the oven and preheat the oven to 350°F (180°C). Lightly butter the bottom and sides of twelve ¾-cup (180-ml) straight-sided ramekins or a 12-cup mini sandwich pan.

In a small bowl, whisk together the flour, baking powder, and salt. In a large bowl, using an electric mixer, beat the butter on medium speed until smooth, about 1 minute. Add the granulated sugar, increase the speed to medium-high, and beat until fluffy and lighter in color, 2–3 minutes. Add the eggs, one at a time, beating well after each addition and adding the vanilla along with the final egg. On low speed, add the flour mixture and mix just until blended.

Divide the batter evenly among the ramekins or mini sandwich cups (a slightly rounded ¼ cup/60 ml each) and spread evenly. Transfer the ramekins or mini sandwich pan to the sheet pan and bake until a toothpick inserted into the center of a cake or two comes out clean, 17–19 minutes.

Transfer the sheet pan to a wire rack and let the cakes cool for 15 minutes. Run a thin-bladed knife around the inside of each ramekin to loosen the cake sides, then invert the ramekin onto a wire rack, lift it off, and turn the cake right side up. If using a mini sandwich pan, loosen the cake sides the same way, then invert the pan onto a rack, lift off the pan, and turn the cakes right side up. (If the cups have a removable bottom, push up to release the cakes.) Let the cakes cool completely.

Recipe continues on the following page

Continued

HISTORY NOTE

The Victoria sponge was made possible by the invention of baking powder by British chemist Alfred Bird in 1843. A favorite of Queen Victoria, it soon became the iconic cake to serve guests with tea.

While the cakes are cooling, ready the filling. In a bowl, using a handheld mixer, beat together the cream and confectioners' sugar on medium speed until stiff peaks form, 2–3 minutes. Fit a piping bag with a small plain or star tip, spoon the whipped cream into the bag, and secure closed. Use right away or refrigerate for up to 2 hours before serving.

Just before serving, using a serrated knife, cut the cakes in half horizontally. Arrange the bottom halves, cut side up, on a work surface. Divide the whipped cream evenly among the cake bottoms, piping small dollops around the edge and then into the center, covering the bottom completely. Spoon about 1 tablespoon of the jam over the cream on each cake bottom, gently spreading it to the edge. Arrange the cake tops, cut side down, on top of the jam. Lightly dust the top of each cake with confectioners' sugar.

MADEIRA CAKE

Popular in the mid-nineteenth century and into the twentieth century, Madeira cake is named for the fortified Portuguese wine that traditionally accompanied it. The wine's taste notes of toasted nuts, caramel, and fruit pair well with the subtle lemon flavor of the cake. Both the wine, often served in a cut-crystal decanter, and the cake, would have been common additions to the Downton tea table.

½ cup (115 g) unsalted butter, melted and cooled, plus room-temperature butter for the pan

¾ cup plus 2 tablespoons (170 g) superfine sugar, plus more for the pan

1 cup (125 g) flour

Grated zest of 1 large or 2 small lemons

½ teaspoon baking powder

3 eggs

½ teaspoon pure vanilla extract

SERVES 8

Preheat the oven to 350°F (180°C). Butter an 8½ x 4½ x 2½-inch (21.5 x 11.5 x 6-cm) loaf pan, then lightly coat with sugar, tapping out the excess.

In a small bowl, whisk together the flour, lemon zest, and baking powder. In a separate, larger bowl, whisk the eggs until thick and creamy. Slowly add the sugar, whisking constantly until fully incorporated. Continuing to whisk constantly, very slowly add the melted butter just until incorporated. (Alternatively, use a handheld mixer on medium-high speed to beat the eggs, then beat in the sugar, and finally the butter.) Carefully fold in the flour mixture just until combined.

Pour the batter into the prepared pan, then get the pan into the oven quickly, before the eggs have a chance to collapse. Bake the cake until a toothpick inserted into the center comes out clean, about 30 minutes. Let cool in the pan on a wire rack for 10 minutes, then carefully turn the cake out onto the rack, turn the cake right side up, and let cool completely before serving.

SIMNEL CAKE

The name of this cake likely derives from the Latin *simla*, which was a flour grade available in ancient Rome used for making a yeast-leavened bread. By the Middle Ages, simnel cake was linked to the Easter holiday, and by the twentieth century, it had evolved into a light fruitcake accented with marzipan, both as a layer inside the cake and for decoration. In this regional adaptation, the cake is topped with a fluted marzipan round and eleven balls symbolizing the apostles of Jesus.

FOR THE MARZIPAN

2¼ cups (225 g) ground almonds

1 cup plus 2 tablespoons (225 g) superfine sugar

1 egg, lightly whisked

1 teaspoon orange flower water

1 teaspoon fresh lemon juice

1 teaspoon apricot or hazelnut schnapps

FOR THE CAKE

½ cup plus 2 tablespoons (145 g) salted butter, at room temperature, plus more for the pan

1¾ cups plus 2 tablespoons (235 g) flour, plus more for the work surface

2 teaspoons ground ginger

½ teaspoon ground cinnamon

½ teaspoon baking powder

¾ cup (150 g) superfine sugar

4 eggs

⅓ cup (80 ml) milk

1½ cups (210 g) dried currants

¼ lb (115 g) dried apricots, chopped

¼ lb (115 g) mixed candied orange and lemon peel, chopped

1 teaspoon grated lemon zest

1 teaspoon grated orange zest

SERVES 12–14

To make the marzipan, in a bowl, combine the ground almonds, sugar, egg, orange flower water, lemon juice, and schnapps and stir together until all the ingredients are well blended and a soft, pliable consistency forms that can be rolled out. Enclose in storage wrap and refrigerate until ready to use.

To make the cake, preheat the oven to 350°F (180°C). Butter the bottom and sides of an 8-inch (20-cm) round cake pan, then line the bottom and sides with a double layer of parchment paper and butter the paper generously.

In a bowl, whisk together the flour, ginger, cinnamon, and baking powder. In a large bowl, using an electric mixer, beat the butter on medium speed until smooth, about 1 minute. Increase the speed to medium-high, add the sugar, and beat until fluffy and lighter in color, 2–3 minutes. On medium speed, add the eggs, one at a time, alternately with the flour mixture in three batches, beginning and ending with the eggs and beating well after each addition. Beat in the milk until blended. Using a wooden spoon, stir in the currants, apricots, candied citrus peel, and citrus zests until evenly distributed.

Divide the marzipan into thirds. On a lightly floured work surface, roll out one-third of the marzipan into an 8-inch (20-cm) round (the diameter of the pan). Pour half of the batter into the prepared pan. Carefully lay the marzipan round on top of the batter in the pan, then pour the remaining batter over the marzipan layer and smooth the top.

Recipe continues on the following page

ATTICUS: *You must have a very sweet tooth.*

She laughs.

ROSE: *No, they're not for me. I give tea to some Russian refugees every Tuesday and Thursday. They love cake.*

ATTICUS: I *love cake!*

~ **SEASON 5, EPISODE 5**

RECIPE NOTE

For a shortcut, substitute 18 oz (500 g) store-bought marzipan for the homemade.

Continued

Bake the cake until a toothpick inserted into the center of the top cake layer (not to the marzipan) comes out clean, about 2 hours. Keep an eye on the top, and if it starts to brown too much, cover it loosely with aluminum foil. Let cool in the pan on a wire rack for 10–15 minutes, then invert the pan onto the rack, lift off the pan, and peel off the parchment. Turn the cake right side up and let cool completely.

If the cake has a domed top, using a serrated knife and a sawing motion, cut off the dome to make the top level, then set the cake on a serving plate. Divide the remaining marzipan in half. Using a rolling pin, roll out half of the marzipan into a 10-inch (25-cm) round and lay the round on top of the cake. Using a thumb and two index fingers, flute the edge of the marzipan round decoratively. Divide the remaining marzipan into 11 equal pieces. Roll each piece into a ball and arrange the balls along the top edge of the cake. Using a kitchen torch, brown the top of the cake (or slip the cake briefly under a preheated broiler). Cut into wedges to serve.

BANBURY TARTS

This iconic British confection, in which a spiced dried-fruit filling is baked in a flaky, traditionally lard-based pastry shell, is an icon of British culinary history. The first known recipe for a Banbury cake appeared in *The English Huswife,* published in 1615, and called for fashioning a sweet yeasted dough and currants into a big, rather elaborate pastry. By the early nineteenth century, individual open-faced tarts featuring currants or raisins were also being made, a size and filling that has remained popular. The tarts were enjoyed across the classes and would have been served both upstairs and downstairs at Downton.

Tart Pastry (page 75)

1½ cups (255 g) raisins

1 cup (240 ml) water

⅔ cup (140 g) sugar

4 soda crackers, finely crushed

2 teaspoons grated lemon zest

2 tablespoons fresh lemon juice

1 egg, lightly whisked

MAKES TWENTY-FOUR
1½-INCH (4-CM)
MINI TARTS

Make the tart pastry and refrigerate as directed.

Have ready a 24-cup mini muffin pan (cups should be about 1¾ inches / 4.5 cm in diameter and ¾ inch / 2 cm deep).

On a lightly floured work surface, roll out the dough about ⅛ inch (3 mm) thick. Using a 2½-inch (6-cm) round cutter, cut out as many rounds as possible. Transfer each round to a muffin cup, gently pressing the dough onto the bottom and up the sides. Gather up the dough scraps, press together, reroll, and cut out more rounds to line the remaining cups. Place the lined pan in the freezer until chilled, about 30 minutes. About 15 minutes before the pastry shells are ready to bake, preheat the oven to 375°F (190°C).

Using a fork, prick the bottom and sides of the pastry lining each cup. Bake until almost golden, about 10 minutes. Let cool completely on a wire rack. Leave the oven set at 375°F (190°C).

In a heavy saucepan over high heat, combine the raisins, water, sugar, crackers, and lemon zest and bring to a boil, stirring to dissolve the sugar. Reduce the heat to low and simmer uncovered, stirring occasionally, until slightly thickened, about 10 minutes. Remove from the heat and stir in the lemon juice and egg until blended.

THOMAS: *Oh, I'm worn out. Give me some tea.*

~ SEASON 6, EPISODE 1

Spoon the raisin mixture into the pastry shells, dividing it evenly and being careful not to spill any onto the pan, which could cause the pastry to stick. Bake until lightly browned on top, about 30 minutes. Remove from the oven, let cool briefly in the pan on a wire rack, and then transfer to the rack. Serve warm.

LEMON TARTS

In the late nineteenth and early twentieth century, lemon curd had a prominent place on the afternoon tea table as the preferred alternative to jam. It was a precious choice as well because, unlike jam, the egg-based curd needed refrigeration for long-term storage. Here, spooned into small, crisp tart shells, it becomes the ideal filling for a quintessential teatime offering.

FOR THE TART PASTRY

1¼ cups (155 g) flour, plus more for the work surface

3 tablespoons sugar

¼ teaspoon salt

10 tablespoons (140 g) cold unsalted butter, cut into tablespoon-size pieces

1 egg yolk

1½ tablespoons ice-cold water, or more if needed

1 cup (250 g) Lemon Curd (page 134)

Fresh berries, thin lemon slices, or edible blossoms, for garnish

Confectioners' sugar, for dusting (optional)

MAKES SIXTEEN
3-INCH (7.5-CM) TARTS

ETIQUETTE NOTE

Small cakes and tarts are often featured on the tea table in *Downton Abbey*. These bite-size treats were considered finger food, which freed guests from using a knife and fork.

To make the tart pastry, in a bowl, whisk together the flour, sugar, and salt. Scatter the butter over the flour mixture and, using your fingertips, two knives, or a pastry blender, work in the butter until the mixture forms large, coarse crumbs. In a small bowl, whisk together the egg yolk and water until blended. Add the egg mixture to the flour mixture and stir and toss gently with a fork until the flour mixture is evenly moistened and forms clumps. Feel the dough; it should be just damp enough to form a rough mass. If necessary, mix in a few more drops of water to achieve the correct consistency. Turn out the dough onto a large piece of storage wrap, cover with the wrap, and shape into a smooth disk. Refrigerate the wrapped dough at least 1 hour or up to overnight.

Have ready sixteen 3-inch (7.5-cm) tartlet pans. On a lightly floured work surface, roll out the dough about ¼ inch (6 mm) thick. Using a round pastry cutter about 3 inches (7.5 cm) in diameter, cut out as many rounds as possible. One at a time, transfer the dough rounds to the tartlet pans, gently pressing the dough onto the bottom and up the sides of each pan and trimming off any overhang. Gather up the scraps, press together, reroll, cut out more rounds, and line the remaining pans. Place the lined pans on a sheet pan and place in the freezer until well chilled, about 30 minutes. About 15 minutes before the pastry shells are ready to bake, preheat the oven to 375°F (190°C).

Using a fork, prick the bottom and sides of the pastry lining each pan. Bake the tartlet shells until golden, 12–14 minutes. Transfer to a wire rack and let cool completely.

Carefully remove the cooled tartlet shells from the pans. Fill the shells with the lemon curd, spreading it in an even layer. Garnish with the fruit or flowers, dust with confectioners' sugar (if using), and serve.

QUINCE TART

In 1275, Edward I planted four quince trees at the Tower of London, thus marking the first recorded appearance of the fragrant fruit being cultivated in England. Recipes for quince jam and jellies, pies, and tarts followed, including an elaborate lattice-top pie published in *The Whole Duty of a Woman* in 1701. At Downton, this simpler tart, in which the filling of quince slices is finished with a glaze of apricot jam, might have drawn on fruit from the estate's gardens.

Tart Pastry (page 75)
2½ cups (600 ml) water
1½ cups (300 g) sugar
1 cinnamon stick, about 2 inches (5 cm) long
1 teaspoon grated lemon zest
3 quinces
½ cup (140 g) apricot jam

SERVES 12

Make the tart pastry and refrigerate as directed.

On a lightly floured work surface, roll out the pastry into a round 12 inches (30 cm) in diameter and about ¼ inch (6 mm) thick. Roll the dough around the pin, center the pin over a 9-inch (23-cm) fluted tart pan with a removable bottom, and unroll the dough, centering it in the pan and allowing the excess to overhang the sides. Press the dough onto the bottom and up the sides of the pan, then trim the edges, allowing a ½-inch (12-mm) overhang. Roll the overhang back over onto itself and press firmly to reinforce the sides of the crust. Place the lined pan in the freezer until chilled, about 30 minutes. About 15 minutes before the tart crust is ready to bake, preheat the oven to 375°F (190°C).

Line the chilled pastry crust with parchment paper and fill with pie weights or dried beans. Bake until the crust is dry to the touch and the edges are beginning to color, about 15 minutes. Remove from the oven and remove the weights and parchment. Lower the oven temperature to 350°F (180°C), return the tart crust to the oven, and bake until golden brown all over, 10–15 minutes longer. Let cool completely in the pan on a wire rack.

To make the filling, in a saucepan over medium heat, combine the water, sugar, cinnamon stick, and lemon zest and bring to a boil, stirring until the sugar dissolves. Reduce the heat to low so the syrup simmers gently.

THOMAS: *What would my Mother say? Me
entertaining the future Earl of Grantham to tea.*

MATTHEW: *War has a way of distinguishing between
the things that matter, and the things that don't.*

~ SEASON 2, EPISODE 1

Peel, halve, and core each quince, then cut each half into 4 wedges. Drop the wedges into the simmering sugar syrup, cover partially, and cook until tender but not mushy, about 1 hour. Remove from the heat and let cool completely. Drain the quinces well, reserving the liquid. Pat the quinces dry.

Cut each quince wedge lengthwise into 2 or 3 slices; set aside. In a small, heavy saucepan, combine the apricot jam with ¼ cup (60 ml) of the reserved quince liquid. Place over high heat, bring to a boil, and boil until thick and syrupy, which should take several minutes. Pass the syrup through a fine-mesh sieve into a small heatproof bowl.

To unmold the cooled tart crust, place the tart pan on a can or overturned bowl and carefully slide the outer ring down. Using a wide offset spatula, loosen the crust from the pan bottom and slide it onto a serving plate.

Brush a thin coating of the warm glaze over the bottom of the cooled tart crust. Arrange the quince slices attractively in the tart crust, overlapping them. Carefully brush the fruit with the remaining glaze and serve as soon as possible.

BAKEWELL TART

This almond-and-jam-filled tart is all but a national treasure in England and is, possibly, the ultimate teatime sweet. Though it's named for the town in Derbyshire where it's likely that it was first introduced, its exact origins are unknown. You can use different jams or fruits and coat it with a sugary glaze, though if you did, Mrs. Patmore would likely call it by another name entirely.

Tart Pastry (page 75)

½ cup (115 g) unsalted butter, at room temperature, plus more for the pan

½ cup (100 g) sugar

½ teaspoon pure almond or vanilla extract (optional)

Pinch of salt

2 eggs, at room temperature

1¼ cups (140 g) almond flour

½ cup (140 g) raspberry or strawberry jam

3 tablespoons sliced almonds (optional)

SERVES 12

Make the tart pastry and refrigerate as directed.

Lightly butter the bottom and sides of a fluted 9-inch (23-cm) tart pan with a removable bottom. On a lightly floured work surface, roll out the pastry into a round 12 inches (30 cm) in diameter and about ¼ inch (6 mm) thick. Roll the dough around the pin, center the pin over the tart pan, and unroll the dough, centering it in the pan and allowing the excess to overhang the sides. Press the dough onto the bottom and up the sides of the pan, then trim the edges, allowing a ½-inch (12-mm) overhang. Roll the overhang back over onto itself and press firmly to reinforce the sides of the crust. Place the lined pan in the freezer while the oven heats, 15–20 minutes.

Preheat the oven to 350°F (180°C).

Line the chilled pastry crust with parchment paper and fill with pie weights or dried beans. Bake until the edges of the crust are light brown, about 20 minutes. Remove from the oven and remove the weights and parchment. Return to the oven and continue baking until the crust is pale golden, 7–9 minutes. Transfer the pan to a wire rack. Leave the oven set at 350°F (180°C).

To make the filling, in a bowl, using an electric mixer, beat together the butter, sugar, almond extract (if using), and salt on medium speed until fluffy and lighter in color, 2–4 minutes. Add the eggs, one at a time, beating well after each addition. On medium-low speed, add the almond flour and beat just until blended.

Recipe continues on the following page

Continued

RECIPE NOTE

The prebaked crust can be cooled completely, covered, and stored at room temperature for up to 1 day before filling and baking.

Spread the jam evenly in the warm tart crust. Drop the filling in small scoopfuls over the jam, then spread carefully and evenly over the jam. Scatter the almonds over the top, if using. Bake the tart until the filling is puffed and browned and the center springs back when lightly pressed, 35–38 minutes. Let cool completely on a wire rack.

To serve, place the tart pan on a can or overturned bowl and carefully slide the outer ring down. Using a wide offset spatula, loosen the crust from the pan bottom and slide the tart onto a serving plate.

STICKY TOFFEE PUDDINGS

Although early British puddings were either savory (meat based) or sweet and were typically boiled in special pudding bags, modern British puddings are commonly dense, moist cakes—often laced with rehydrated dried fruits—that are either steamed or baked. These toffee-topped puddings did not appear on the English table until the late twentieth century, though similar small puddings baked in ramekins would not have been uncommon in Mrs. Patmore's kitchen.

FOR THE PUDDINGS

4 tablespoons (60 g) unsalted butter, at room temperature, plus more for the custard cups

1 cup (125 g) flour, plus more for the custard cups

½ cup (70 g) pitted and finely chopped dates

¾ teaspoon baking soda

¾ cup (180 ml) boiling water

1¼ teaspoons baking powder

½ teaspoon salt

¾ cup (155 g) firmly packed dark brown sugar

2 eggs

2 teaspoons pure vanilla extract

FOR THE SAUCE

4 tablespoons (60 g) unsalted butter

¾ cup (155 g) firmly packed dark brown sugar

¾ cup (180 ml) heavy cream

2 teaspoons pure vanilla extract

Pinch of salt

MAKES 8 PUDDINGS

To make the puddings, preheat the oven to 350°F (180°C). Butter eight ½-cup (120-ml) custard cups or ramekins, then dust with flour, tapping out the excess. Place on a sheet pan.

In a small heatproof bowl, combine the dates, baking soda, and boiling water. Let stand until cool, about 10 minutes.

In a bowl, whisk together the flour, baking powder, and salt. In a large bowl, using an electric mixer, beat together the butter and brown sugar on medium speed until smooth and lighter in color, about 3 minutes. Add the eggs, one at a time, beating well after each addition and adding the vanilla with the final egg. Add the flour mixture and stir with a wooden spoon until well blended. Add the date mixture and stir until evenly distributed. The batter will be thin. Divide the batter evenly among the prepared custard cups, filling them about two-thirds full.

Bake the puddings until they are puffed and a toothpick inserted into the center comes out clean, about 20 minutes.

Meanwhile, make the sauce. In a saucepan over medium heat, melt the butter. Add the brown sugar and cream and whisk until the sauce becomes sticky, about 5 minutes. Stir in the vanilla and salt.

When the puddings are ready, remove from the oven and let cool for 5 minutes. Run a thin-bladed knife around the inside of each custard cup to loosen the pudding sides and invert the warm puddings onto individual plates. Top each pudding with a big spoonful of the toffee sauce, letting it run down the sides and onto the plate. Serve right away.

STEAMED FIGGY PUDDING

The Forme of Cury, published circa 1390, is among England's oldest cookbooks. In it is a recipe for figgy pudding's ancestor, fygey. Along with figs and raisins, it calls for "almande blanched [and] grynde . . . water and wyne, powdour gyngur and hony clarified" to be boiled, salted, and then served. Offered at the end of a meal or at teatime, the dense steamed pudding is a true British classic, here presented in a modern version.

7 tablespoons (100 g) unsalted butter, at room temperature, plus more for the mold

1½ cups (225 g) dried figs, stemmed

½ cup (70 g) dried currants

2 cups (480 ml) water

8 slices good-quality white sandwich bread, crusts removed and bread torn into pea-size crumbs

1¼ cups (155 g) flour

½ cup (100 g) firmly packed dark brown sugar

3 eggs

1 cup (240 ml) milk

1 teaspoon pure vanilla extract

2 tablespoons chopped candied orange peel

1 tablespoon grated orange zest

FOR THE WHIPPED CREAM

1½ cups (350 ml) heavy cream

¼ cup (50 g) granulated sugar

SERVES 8–10

Butter a 1½-quart (1.5-l) steamed pudding mold.

In a small saucepan over medium-high heat, combine the figs, currants, and water and bring to a boil. Reduce the heat to low and simmer, uncovered, until the figs are tender but still hold their shape, about 20 minutes. Remove from the heat.

Using a slotted spoon, transfer the figs and currants to a bowl; reserve the cooking liquid. Cut 8–10 of the figs in half lengthwise and press them, cut side down, in a decorative pattern in the prepared mold. Chop the remaining figs.

In a medium bowl, whisk together the bread crumbs and flour. In a large bowl, using an electric mixer, beat the butter on medium speed until smooth, about 1 minute. Increase the speed to medium-high, add the brown sugar, and beat until fluffy, 2–3 minutes. Add the eggs, one at a time, beating well after each addition. Add the milk and vanilla and beat until incorporated. Switch to a rubber spatula and stir in the orange peel, orange zest, currants, and chopped figs. Still using the spatula, fold half of the flour mixture into the egg mixture just until blended, then fold in the remaining flour mixture until no dry streaks remain. Pour the batter into the prepared mold and fasten the lid.

Set a rack on the bottom of a large pot with a lid and put the mold on the rack. Pour boiling water into the pot to reach halfway up the sides of the mold. Bring to a boil over high heat, reduce the heat to medium-low, cover, and slowly steam at a gentle boil for 2 hours. Check the water level every now and again and replenish with boiling water as needed to maintain the original level.

When the pudding is ready, carefully remove the mold from the pot and let stand for 15 minutes.

While the pudding rests, make the whipped cream and the syrup. In a bowl, using the electric mixer, beat the cream on medium speed until soft peaks form. Slowly add the granulated sugar while continuing to beat until stiff peaks form. Cover and refrigerate until serving.

For the syrup, in a small saucepan over high heat, bring the reserved fig liquid to a boil and boil until reduced to ½ cup (120 ml), about 5 minutes. Keep warm.

Uncover the mold, invert it onto a serving platter, and then tap the mold gently to release the pudding. To serve, cut into wedges and transfer to individual plates. Drizzle a little syrup alongside each wedge and top with the whipped cream.

BUTTERFLY CAKES

Posher British cousins of the traditional American cupcake, these pretty petite cakes are topped with a dollop of whipped cream, a spot of jam, and a charming set of "wings" fashioned from the domed cake tops—a perfect small and delicate bite for any teatime tray.

FOR THE CAKES

1⅔ cups (215 g) flour

1¼ teaspoons baking powder

½ teaspoon salt

½ cup (115 g) unsalted butter, at room temperature

¾ cup (150 g) granulated sugar

2 eggs, at room temperature

½ teaspoon pure vanilla extract

½ cup (120 ml) milk

FOR THE TOPPING

½ cup (120 ml) heavy cream

1 tablespoon confectioners' sugar, plus more for dusting (optional)

1 tablespoon strawberry or raspberry jam

MAKES 12 SMALL CAKES

To make the cakes, preheat the oven to 350°F (180°C). Line 12 standard muffin cups with paper liners.

In a small bowl, whisk together the flour, baking powder, and salt. In a large bowl, using an electric mixer, beat the butter on medium speed until smooth, about 1 minute. Add the granulated sugar, increase the speed to medium-high, and beat until fluffy and lighter in color, 2–3 minutes. Add the eggs, one at a time, beating well after each addition and adding the vanilla with the final egg. On low speed, add about half of the flour mixture and mix just until blended, then add the milk and again mix until blended. Add the remaining flour mixture and mix just until blended.

Divide the batter evenly among the prepared cups and spread evenly. Bake until a toothpick inserted into the center of a cake or two comes out clean, 17–19 minutes. Let cool in the pan on a wire rack for 15 minutes. Lift the cakes from the pan and arrange, top side up, on the rack. Let cool completely.

To make the topping, in a bowl, using a handheld mixer, beat together the cream and confectioners' sugar on medium speed until stiff peaks form, 2–3 minutes. Use right away or cover and refrigerate up to 2 hours before serving.

Just before serving, using a serrated knife, cut off the domed top from each cake and cut in half crosswise to form the "wings." Spoon (or pipe with a plain tip) some of the whipped cream onto the center of the cupcake. Put a small dollop (about ¼ teaspoon) of the jam onto the center of the whipped cream. Gently push 2 "wings," cut side down and at a slight angle, into the cream, positioning them on either side of the jam. Lightly dust the top of each cake with confectioners' sugar, if desired.

ROSE & VANILLA FAIRY CAKES

Fairy cakes are a British teatime classic and a favorite of children. Similar to modern cupcakes though smaller, the delicate cakes are traditionally bite-size sponge cakes dressed up with whimsical decorations. Nowadays, most fairy cakes are cupcake size and are often a butter cake rather than a sponge cake. Embellish these petite pink-frosted treats with pistachios and confectioners' sugar as suggested, or decorate them with sparkling sugar, frosting flowers, rose petals, or other edible blossoms.

FOR THE CAKES

1½ cups (185 g) self-rising flour

Pinch of kosher salt

¾ cup (170 g) unsalted butter

¾ cup (150 g) granulated sugar

1 tablespoon rose water

1½ teaspoons pure vanilla extract

3 eggs

FOR THE FROSTING

½ cup (115 g) unsalted butter, at cool room temperature

3 cups (340 g) confectioners' sugar, sifted

Pinch of kosher salt

1 tablespoon rose water

1 teaspoon pure vanilla extract

3 drops pink food coloring

2 tablespoons finely chopped pistachios (optional)

Confectioners' sugar, for dusting (optional)

MAKES 12 SMALL CAKES

To make the cakes, preheat the oven to 350°F (180°C). Line 12 standard muffin cups with paper liners.

Sift together the flour and salt into a small bowl. In a large bowl, using an electric mixer, beat together the butter and granulated sugar on medium-high speed until light and fluffy, about 3 minutes. Beat in the rose water and vanilla until blended. On medium speed, add the eggs, one at a time, beating well after each addition. On low speed, gradually add the flour mixture, mixing just until incorporated.

Spoon the batter into the prepared muffin cups, dividing it evenly. Bake until golden and a toothpick inserted into the center of a cake or two comes out clean, 15–20 minutes. Let cool completely in the pan on a wire rack, then remove from the pan.

To make the frosting, in a bowl, using the electric mixer, beat together the butter, confectioners' sugar, and salt on medium speed until smooth and fluffy, 2–3 minutes. Add the rose water, vanilla, and food coloring and beat until evenly colored.

Fit a piping bag with a small star tip, spoon the frosting into the bag, and secure closed. Pipe the frosting onto the top of each cupcake. Sprinkle with the pistachios and dust with confectioners' sugar (if using) and serve.

APPLE CRUMBLE CAKE

There were numerous apple varieties available in Edwardian England, and the fruit was extremely popular for use in both cooking and baking. When you can, select heirloom varieties, which are both tarter and more versatile. Granny Smith and Cox's Orange Pippin are good choices, as is the Braeburn. Bramley is the best-known cooking variety in Britain and a sound bet for any baking recipe.

FOR THE CAKE

Unsalted butter, for the pan

3 cups (375 g) flour, plus more for the pan

1 teaspoon baking soda

1 teaspoon ground cinnamon

¼ teaspoon salt

1 cup (200 g) granulated sugar

1 cup (210 g) firmly packed light brown sugar

¾ cup (180 ml) canola oil

¾ cup (170 g) unsweetened applesauce

3 eggs

3 baking apples, peeled, cored, and cut into cubes

FOR THE TOPPING

1 cup (125 g) flour

½ cup (115 g) cold unsalted butter, cut into cubes

½ cup (100 g) firmly packed light brown sugar

SERVES 12

To make the cake, preheat the oven to 350°F (180°C). Lightly butter a 9 x 13-inch (23 x 33-cm) baking pan, then dust with flour, tapping out the excess.

In a large bowl, stir together the flour, baking soda, cinnamon, and salt. In a medium bowl, whisk together both sugars, the oil, applesauce, and eggs until blended. Make a well in the center of the flour mixture, add the sugar mixture to the well, and stir just until smooth. Add the apples and stir until evenly distributed. Spread the batter in the prepared pan, smoothing the top.

To make the topping, in a bowl, combine the flour, butter, and brown sugar. Using your fingers, work the ingredients together just until evenly mixed. Press the mixture together into a ball and then separate with your fingers into coarse crumbs. Sprinkle the crumbs evenly over the top of the cake.

Bake the cake until a toothpick inserted into the center comes out clean, about 1 hour. Let cool completely in the pan on a wire rack. Cut into squares and serve.

RECIPE NOTE

If using a glass baking dish, lower the oven temperature to 325°F (165°C).

DUNDEE CAKE

Rumor has it that Mary, Queen of Scots, did not like candied cherries in her cakes, and the inception of this cake was the result of a workaround that swapped in blanched almonds for the customary stone fruit. James Keiller & Sons, a marmalade company in Dundee, Scotland, coined the name Dundee cake to describe the modern version, which it developed and began mass-producing in the mid-nineteenth century.

1 lb (450 g) mixed golden and dark raisins

6 tablespoons (90 ml) Scotch whisky

1 cup (225 g) butter, at room temperature, plus more for the pan

1 cup (210 g) firmly packed Demerara sugar

Pinch of salt

4 eggs

2¼ cups (280 g) flour

¼ teaspoon ground cinnamon

¼ teaspoon ground nutmeg

1 cup plus 2 tablespoons (115 g) ground almonds

½ cup (160 g) orange marmalade

Grated zest of 2 oranges

⅔ cup (95 g) whole blanched almonds, for decorating

SERVES 8–10

In a saucepan over low heat, combine the raisins and whisky and heat, stirring once or twice, until hot, 10–15 minutes. Remove from the heat and let steep for 2 hours.

Preheat the oven to 325°F (165°C). Butter the bottom and sides of a 9-inch (23-cm) round cake pan. Line the bottom with parchment paper and butter the parchment.

In a large bowl, using an electric mixer, beat the butter on medium speed until smooth, about 1 minute. Increase the speed to medium-high, add the sugar and salt, and beat until fluffy and lighter in color, 2–3 minutes. Add the eggs, one at a time, together with a spoonful of the flour with the first egg to stop the mix from curdling, beating well after each addition. Beat in the remaining flour and the cinnamon and nutmeg until incorporated. Using a wooden spoon, stir in the raisins and whisky, the ground almonds, marmalade, and orange zest until evenly distributed.

Transfer the batter to the prepared pan, spread evenly, and smooth the top. Arrange the whole blanched almonds on top in concentric circles, with the pointed end of each nut directed toward the center. Bake the cake until a toothpick inserted into the center comes out clean, 1½–1¾ hours. Let cool completely in the pan on a wire rack, then invert the pan onto the rack, lift off the pan, and peel off the parchment. Transfer the cake right side up to a serving plate and serve.

PARKIN

Warm spices, treacle, and oats form the basis of the beloved parkin cake, a gingerbread-like treat commonly eaten during the winter months. The amount of black treacle and golden syrup added varies from county to county, but the sticky, chewy, slightly nubby texture stays the same. In the United States, these two products can be found in well-stocked markets or online. Lyle's (Tate & Lyle) makes quality versions of both. If black treacle is not available, blackstrap molasses can be substituted in the same amount. Likewise, medium oats (not rolled oats) can be purchased online, or steel cut oats can be processed into a coarse meal and used as a substitute, as is done here.

½ cup (115 g) unsalted butter, plus more for the pan

1¼ cups (160 g) flour, plus more for the pan

¾ cup (150 g) firmly packed dark brown sugar

½ cup (170 g) black treacle or blackstrap molasses

½ cup (170 g) golden syrup

3 tablespoons milk

1 cup (175 g) steel cut oats

2 teaspoons baking powder

2 teaspoons ground ginger

1½ teaspoons mixed spice or pumpkin pie spice

¼ teaspoon salt

1 egg

SERVES 12

Preheat the oven to 300°F (150°C). Lightly butter the bottom and sides of an 8-inch (20-cm) square pan. Line the bottom with parchment paper, lightly butter the parchment, and then dust the bottom and sides with flour, tapping out the excess.

In a saucepan over medium heat, combine the butter, brown sugar, treacle, golden syrup, and milk and cook, stirring, until the butter and sugar are melted and the mixture is smooth, 4–6 minutes. Remove the pan from the heat and let cool for 5 minutes.

In a food processor, pulse the oats until they are coarsely chopped (there will be some finely ground and some coarse pieces), 1–2 minutes. Transfer to a bowl, add the flour, baking powder, ginger, mixed spice, and salt, and whisk until blended. Scrape the molasses mixture into the oat-flour mixture, add the egg, and stir until well blended.

Scrape the batter into the prepared pan and spread evenly. Bake until a toothpick inserted into the center of the cake comes out with only a few moist crumbs clinging to it, 75–80 minutes. The center will be slightly lower than the edges. Let cool in the pan on a wire rack for 20 minutes, then turn the cake out of the pan, peel off the parchment, turn right side up, and let cool completely.

Cut into small squares and store in an airtight container at room temperature for up to 1 week. The flavor and texture are best when the cake is made at least 3 days before serving.

SPICY DARK GINGERBREAD

Although the small English town of Market Drayton claims the title of Home of Gingerbread, the spice-packed cake more likely entered Europe in the late tenth century, thanks to an Armenian monk who settled in north-central France, where he taught the locals how to make it. By the time gingerbread found its way to Market Drayton, where it was first reportedly baked in the early 1790s, treacle and flour had replaced the honey and bread crumbs of the medieval formula and eggs and butter had found their way into the batter, yielding a richer, lighter cake that later proved a perfect accompaniment to tea.

3 cups (375 g) flour

2 tablespoons ground ginger

1 teaspoon ground cinnamon

1 teaspoon ground allspice

1 teaspoon baking soda

½ teaspoon kosher salt

¼ cup (35 g) peeled and grated fresh ginger

1 cup (225 g) unsalted butter, at room temperature

1 cup (225 g) firmly packed light brown sugar

1 egg

1 cup (340 g) light molasses

1 cup (240 ml) buttermilk

Whipped cream, for serving (optional)

SERVES 10–12

Preheat the oven to 350°F (180°C). Butter two 8½ x 4½ x 2½-inch (21.5 x 11.5 x 6-cm) loaf pans or a 10-inch (25-cm) Bundt pan, then lightly dust with flour, tapping out the excess.

In a large bowl, whisk together the flour, ground ginger, cinnamon, allspice, baking soda, salt, and fresh ginger. In another large bowl, using an electric mixer, beat the butter on medium speed until smooth, about 1 minute. Increase the speed to medium-high, add the brown sugar, and beat until light and creamy, 2–3 minutes. Add the egg and beat until incorporated, then add the molasses and beat until well blended, about 2 minutes. On low speed, add the flour mixture in three batches alternately with the buttermilk in two batches, beginning and ending with the flour mixture and mixing well after each addition. Transfer the batter to the prepared pan(s) and smooth the surface.

Bake the cake until a toothpick inserted into the center comes out clean, about 50 minutes. Let cool in the pan(s) on a wire rack for 10 minutes. Run a thin-bladed knife around the inside of the pan(s) to loosen any stuck edges, then turn the cake(s) out of the pan(s) onto the rack. (If using loaf pans, turn the cakes right side up; if using a Bundt pan, leave the cake inverted.) Let cool for at least 15 minutes before serving. Accompany each slice with whipped cream, if you like.

BARA BRITH

The name of this Welsh teatime cakelike bread translates to "mottled bread" or "speckled bread," a nod to the copious amount of dried fruit in the loaf. The texture is moist and dense, and the sweetness is on the lighter side, with a touch of orange marmalade flavor. Here only currants are used, but a mixture of dried fruits—candied citrus peel, dark and golden raisins, cranberries—is common, with any larger pieces cut into bite-size bits. Soak the fruit in a strong black tea—Earl Grey or Irish breakfast is a good choice—for at least eight hours, so it absorbs as much of the tea as possible. This bread is delicious toasted and spread with butter.

1⅔ cups (240 g) dried currants

½ cup (120 ml) hot strong black tea

Unsalted butter, for the pan and for serving

1¾ cups (225 g) flour, plus more for the pan

⅔ cup (140 g) firmly packed dark brown sugar

2 teaspoons baking powder

1½ teaspoons mixed spice or pumpkin pie spice

¼ teaspoon salt

¼ cup (60 ml) water

1 egg, lightly whisked

2 tablespoons orange marmalade

SERVES 8–12

In a bowl, combine the currants and hot tea. Let stand, stirring occasionally, until the fruit is softened and the liquid is almost absorbed, 8–12 hours.

Preheat the oven to 325°F (165°C). Lightly butter an 8½ x 4½ x 2½-inch (21.5 x 11.5 x 6-cm) loaf pan, then dust with flour, tapping out the excess.

In a bowl, whisk together the flour, brown sugar, baking powder, mixed spice, and salt. Add the currants and any remaining soaking liquid, the water, egg, and marmalade and stir until well blended.

Transfer the batter to the prepared pan and spread evenly. Bake until a toothpick inserted into the center of the cake comes out clean, 72–75 minutes. Let cool in the pan on a wire rack for 20 minutes, then turn out onto the rack, turn right side up, and let cool completely.

To serve, cut into thick slices and serve at room temperature or toasted with butter.

CHOCOLATE-HAZELNUT DACQUOISE

The term *dacquoise* refers to both the baked layers of nut meringue and the cake itself—yet another British import from the kitchens of French pastry chefs in the nineteenth century. Here, a single large dacquoise is made, suitable for cutting into narrow wedges for teatime. But the same ingredients can be fashioned into small meringues, which can be layered with the buttercream and served as bite-size treats.

FOR THE DACQUOISE

Unsalted butter and flour, for the pans

1⅓ cups (185 g) plus ¼ cup (35 g) hazelnuts, skinned and toasted

1 cup (200 g) granulated sugar

3 tablespoons Dutch-process cocoa powder

2 tablespoons cornstarch

6 egg whites, at room temperature

1 teaspoon pure vanilla extract

FOR THE BUTTERCREAM

2 cups (450 g) unsalted butter, at room temperature

3 cups (340 g) confectioners' sugar

1 teaspoon pure vanilla extract

1 teaspoon hazelnut extract

⅛ teaspoon kosher salt

FOR THE GANACHE

6 oz (170 g) bittersweet or semisweet chocolate, finely chopped

2 tablespoons unsalted butter

½ cup (120 ml) heavy cream

Confectioners' sugar, for dusting

SERVES 8–10

To make the dacquoise, preheat the oven to 300°F (150°C). Lightly butter the bottom and sides of two 11 x 17-inch (28 x 43-cm) sheet pans. Cut a sheet of parchment paper to fit the bottom of each pan. Using an 8-inch (20-cm) round cake pan as a guide, trace two circles on each parchment sheet. Place each sheet, circles side down, on a prepared pan. Butter the paper, then flour the bottom and sides of the pan, tapping out the excess. You should be able to see the traced circles through the paper.

In a food processor or blender, combine 1⅓ cups (185 g) of the hazelnuts, ½ cup (100 g) of the granulated sugar, the cocoa powder, and the cornstarch and process until the nuts are ground to a powder.

In a large bowl, using an electric mixer, beat the egg whites on medium-high speed until they form soft peaks and have tripled in volume. With the mixer still on medium-high speed, slowly pour in the remaining ½ cup (100 g) granulated sugar and the vanilla and beat until the whites are stiff and glossy. Be careful not to overwhip the whites, or they will be dry and powdery.

Pour the hazelnut-sugar mixture over the beaten egg whites. Using a rubber spatula, fold in the nut mixture gently and quickly, with as few strokes as possible. Fit a piping bag with a ½-inch (12-mm) plain tip, spoon some of the batter into it, and secure closed.

Holding the bag upright just above a prepared pan and starting in the middle of a circle, pipe spirals of the batter until you reach the edge of the circle, covering the circle completely. Repeat to cover the second circle on the pan. Refill the bag as necessary and pipe the batter onto the circles on the second pan the same way, piping the fourth circle as full as possible with the batter you have left.

Bake the layers until they are crisp, dry, and beginning to brown, 50–60 minutes. They will feel crisp on top when done, but they might give a little while they are still warm. Let cool completely on the pans on wire racks. The layers will become crisp as they cool.

To make the buttercream, in a bowl, using the electric mixer on medium speed, beat the butter until smooth, about 2 minutes. Add the confectioners' sugar, vanilla and hazelnut extracts, and salt, increase the speed to medium-high, and beat until combined, stopping the mixer to scrape down the sides of the bowl as needed. Cover and refrigerate.

To make the ganache, combine the chocolate and butter in a heatproof bowl. In a small saucepan over medium-high heat, bring the cream just to a boil. Remove the cream from the heat and immediately pour it over the chocolate and butter, then whisk until the chocolate and butter melt and are smooth. Let cool until spreadable.

To assemble the cake, gently peel the cooled layers away from the parchment paper. Using a serrated knife and a sawing motion, trim the 3 solid layers so they are exactly the same size. Using a rolling pin, crush any trimmings along with the fourth round and transfer to a bowl. Finely chop the remaining ¼ cup (35 g) hazelnuts and add to the crushed trimmings. Set aside.

Place 1 layer on a large platter. Using an icing spatula, spread about ⅓ cup (80 g) buttercream in a thin, even layer on top. Place a second layer on top of the buttercream and spread with the same amount of buttercream. Place the third layer on top. Using as much of the remaining buttercream as needed, spread the top and sides of the cake with a thin coating, smoothing it as evenly as possible.

Coat the entire cake with the crumb-nut mixture, gently pressing it against the sides and top with your hands. Using a fine-mesh sieve, sift a light dusting of confectioners' sugar over the top. If desired, fit a clean piping bag with a small star tip, spoon any remaining buttercream into it, secure closed, and pipe a border of rosettes on the top of the cake. Slip a wide metal spatula underneath the cake and transfer it to a serving plate.

The cake can be cut right away, but it is easier to cut if it is first allowed to soften for several hours in the refrigerator. It will keep, well covered in the refrigerator, for up to 2 days. Slice into wedges with a sharp chef's knife or a serrated knife and serve at room temperature.

ALMOND CAKE

Almonds have been imported by the British since medieval times and have long been a common addition to cake recipes. Here, ground almonds and almond extract impart a bold flavor to this rich, moist, nutty teatime favorite. In late spring, when cherries are in season, add them to the table to echo the kirsch in the hot syrup used to infuse the warm cake.

FOR THE CAKE
Unsalted butter, for the pan
1 cup (100 g) ground almonds
½ cup (60 g) flour
1 teaspoon baking powder
1¼ cups (250 g) granulated sugar
6 eggs, separated, at room temperature
Grated zest of 1 lemon
1 teaspoon pure almond extract

FOR THE SYRUP
3 tablespoons kirsch
1 tablespoon fresh lemon juice
2 tablespoons granulated sugar

Confectioners' sugar, for dusting

SERVES 8–10

Preheat the oven to 325°F (165°C). Butter the bottom and sides of a 9-inch (23-cm) springform pan and line the bottom with parchment paper.

To make the cake, in a medium bowl, whisk together the ground almonds, flour, and baking powder. In a large bowl, using an electric mixer, beat together the sugar, egg yolks, and lemon zest on medium speed until thick and pale, about 10 minutes. Add the ground almond mixture and almond extract and stir with a wooden spoon to blend well.

In a bowl, using clean beaters, beat the egg whites on medium-high speed until soft peaks form. Using a rubber spatula, fold the beaten whites into the egg yolk mixture just until no white streaks remain.

Pour the batter into the prepared pan and gently smooth the top. Bake the cake until the top springs back when lightly touched, about 1 hour. Transfer the pan to a wire rack and remove the pan sides.

To make the syrup, in a small saucepan over medium heat, combine the kirsch, lemon juice, and granulated sugar and heat, stirring, until the sugar dissolves and the mixture is hot. Remove from the heat and brush the hot syrup gently and evenly over the hot cake. Let the cake cool completely.

Just before serving, lightly dust the top of the cake with confectioners' sugar.

WALNUT TORTE

In the 1870s, afternoon tea at home was enjoyed by both the rich and the poor, with the lower classes especially keen to take up a custom that was enjoyed by the gentry. By the Edwardian period, tearooms were popping up everywhere, and afternoon tea was no longer something done only at home. The sweets at these new outposts varied according to how fancy the surroundings were. This classic nut torte would not have been out of place in the finest tearooms.

1¾ cups (200 g) walnut or pecan pieces

2 tablespoons flour

¼ teaspoon salt

6 eggs, separated, at room temperature

⅔ cup (140 g) sugar

SERVES 10–12

Preheat the oven to 325°F (165°C). Line the bottom of a 9-inch (23-cm) round cake pan with parchment paper.

In a food processor, combine the walnuts, flour, and salt and process until the nuts are finely ground; do not overprocess.

In a large bowl, using an electric mixer, beat together the egg yolks and ⅓ cup (70 g) of the sugar on medium-high speed until pale and thick, 3–5 minutes. Using a rubber spatula, fold the walnut mixture into the egg yolk mixture just until evenly mixed.

In a large bowl, using clean beaters, beat the egg whites on medium speed until they start to foam. Add about one-third of the remaining sugar and beat until the whites are opaque. Add about half of the remaining sugar and continue to beat until the whites start to increase in volume and become firm. Add the remaining sugar, increase the speed to high, and beat until the whites form soft peaks but still look wet. Using the spatula, fold one-third of the whites into the walnut mixture, then gently fold in the remaining whites just until no white streaks remain.

Transfer the batter to the prepared pan and smooth the top. Bake the torte until lightly browned and a toothpick inserted into the center comes out clean, 35–40 minutes. Let cool completely in the pan on a wire rack.

Run a thin-bladed knife around the inside of the pan to loosen the torte sides, then invert the pan onto a serving plate, lift off the pan, and peel off the parchment. Turn the torte right side up on the plate and cut into wedges to serve.

PLUM BUTTER CAKE

With the invention of modern baking powder in England in 1843, a wealth of new baking opportunities suddenly became possible. Even the traditional English pound cake, made with equal parts butter, flour, sugar, and eggs, was given a shot of the modern leavener, resulting in the lighter, fluffier butter cake. For this rich teatime offering, the Downton kitchen would have turned to the Victoria, Farleigh damson, or another good cooking plum, perhaps from the estate's own garden.

1 cup (225 g) unsalted butter, at room temperature, plus more for the pan

1½ cups (185 g) flour

1 teaspoon baking powder

¼ teaspoon salt

¾ cup (150 g) plus 1 tablespoon sugar

2 eggs

6–8 plums, about 1 lb (450 g), pitted and thickly sliced

¼ teaspoon ground cinnamon

SERVES 6

Position a rack in the lower third of the oven and preheat the oven to 350°F (180°C). Butter a 9-inch (23-cm) round or 8-inch (20-cm) square cake pan. Line the bottom with parchment paper and butter the parchment.

Sift together the flour, baking powder, and salt into a bowl. In another bowl, using an electric mixer, beat the butter on medium speed until smooth, about 1 minute. Increase the speed to medium-high, add ¾ cup (140 g) of the sugar, and beat until fluffy and lighter in color, 2–3 minutes. Add the eggs, one at a time, beating well after each addition. On low speed, add the flour mixture and mix just until blended.

Transfer the batter to the prepared pan, spread evenly, and smooth the top. Poke the plum slices into the batter, placing them close together and covering the top completely. In a small bowl, stir together the cinnamon and the remaining 1 tablespoon sugar and sprinkle evenly over the plums.

Bake the cake until the top is golden, the edges pull away from the pan, and a toothpick inserted into the center comes out clean, 50–60 minutes. Let cool in the pan on a wire rack for about 30 minutes before serving. Serve warm.

LEMON DRIZZLE CAKE

Warne's Model Cookery and Housekeeping Book, published in **1868** in both London and
New York, contains one of the earliest recipes for lemon cake, which calls for just four
ingredients: eggs, flour, sugar, and grated lemon peel. A staple of tearooms in the National
Trust properties and regularly voted among the top ten favorite cakes in Britain, this
deliciously sticky, moist version is slightly more elaborate yet just as traditional.

FOR THE CAKE

½ cup (115 g) unsalted butter,
at room temperature,
plus more for the pan

1½ cups (185 g) flour,
plus more for the pan

1 teaspoon baking powder

½ teaspoon salt

¾ cup (150 g) granulated
sugar

1 tablespoon grated
lemon zest

3 eggs

½ cup (120 ml) milk

1 teaspoon pure
vanilla extract

FOR THE SYRUP

3 tablespoons fresh
lemon juice

3 tablespoons
granulated sugar

FOR THE GLAZE

½ cup (60 g) confectioners'
sugar

1 tablespoon fresh
lemon juice

SERVES 8

To make the cake, preheat the oven to 375°F (190°C). Butter a
9 x 5 x 3-inch (23 x 13 x 7.5-cm) loaf pan, then dust with flour,
tapping out the excess.

Sift together the flour, baking powder, and salt into a bowl. In a large
bowl, using an electric mixer, beat together the butter, granulated
sugar, and lemon zest on medium-high speed until fluffy and lighter
in color, about 3 minutes. Add the eggs, one at a time, beating well
after each addition. Add the milk and vanilla and beat until blended.
On low speed, add the flour mixture and beat just until blended.

Transfer the batter to the prepared pan and smooth the surface.
Bake the cake until golden brown and a toothpick inserted into the
center comes out clean, about 55 minutes. Let the cake cool in the
pan on a wire rack for a few minutes, then turn it out onto the rack.
Turn the cake on its side to cool while you make the syrup.

To make the syrup, in a small saucepan over medium heat, combine
the lemon juice and granulated sugar. Bring to a simmer, stirring to
dissolve the sugar, and then simmer until syrupy, about 2 minutes.
Remove from the heat.

Using a long wooden skewer, pierce the sides and the bottom of the
warm cake, making the holes about 1 inch (2.5 cm) apart and 1 inch
(2.5 cm) deep. Brush the sides and bottom of the cake generously
with the syrup, making sure it seeps into the holes.

To make the glaze, in a small bowl, whisk together the confectioners'
sugar and lemon juice until smooth. When the cake is cool, turn it
right side up on a serving plate and drizzle the glaze over the top.
Let stand until the glaze is set, about 15 minutes, and serve.

ECCLES CAKES

The first official Eccles cakes were sold in 1793 from a bakery in the town of Eccles, in Lancashire. The light, flaky pastry for these small currant-filled sweets is a cross between a pie dough and a puff pastry dough, with just a hint of sweetness. It's said that these gems are typically 40 percent filling and 60 percent pastry, to ensure the perfect balance of sweet fruit and crispy, buttery pastry.

FOR THE PASTRY

2 cups (250 g) flour, plus more for the work surface and rolling

2 tablespoons granulated sugar

½ teaspoon salt

1 cup (225 g) cold unsalted butter, diced

⅓ cup (80 ml) ice-cold water

FOR THE FILLING

2 tablespoons firmly packed light brown sugar

2 tablespoons unsalted butter, at very soft room temperature

1 teaspoon mixed spice or pumpkin pie spice

¼ teaspoon grated lemon zest

¼ teaspoon grated orange zest

⅔ cup (95 g) dried currants

¼ cup (35 g) chopped mixed candied orange and lemon peel

1 tablespoon brandy or Cognac (optional)

FOR ASSEMBLY

1 egg white, lightly whisked

Demerara sugar, for sprinkling (optional)

MAKES 16 CAKES

To make the pastry, in a food processor, combine the flour, sugar, and salt and process until blended, about 5 seconds. Scatter the butter over the flour mixture and process until the butter is coated and slightly chopped, about 2 seconds. Sprinkle the water over the flour and butter and process until the dough comes together in small, moist crumbs, 7–10 seconds.

Scrape the dough onto a lightly floured work surface and shape into a rough rectangle. Roll out into a 6 x 18-inch (15 x 45-cm) rectangle, lightly flouring the dough and work surface as needed. The edges will be ragged. Fold the short ends toward each other so they meet in the middle. Fold the dough crosswise in half to make a 4½ x 6-inch (11.5 x 15-cm) rectangle. Rotate the dough so the seam is on the right and repeat the rolling and folding technique. Divide the dough crosswise into 2 equal rectangles (about 10½ oz/300 g) each. Wrap the rectangles in storage wrap and refrigerate until well chilled, about 2 hours or up to overnight.

To make the filling, in a bowl, combine the brown sugar, butter, mixed spice, and lemon and orange zest and, using a rubber spatula, mix until well blended. Add the currants, candied peel, and brandy (if using) and stir until well blended. Divide the mixture into 16 small mounds (about 2 teaspoons each), arrange on a plate, and flatten slightly (about 1½ inches/4 cm in diameter). Cover and refrigerate for at least 20 minutes or up to overnight.

Recipe continues on the following page

MOLESLEY: *It's hard to cope with three ladies at once.*
What with the tweeds and evening dresses and tea gowns, an' all.

MRS. HUGHES: *Tea gowns? We're not in the 1890s now, Mr. Molesley.*

CARSON: *More's the pity.*

~ SEASON 5, EPISODE 9

Continued

Preheat the oven to 400°F (200°C). Line a sheet pan with parchment paper.

To assemble the cakes, place half of the pastry dough on a lightly floured work surface and roll out ³⁄₁₆ inch (5 mm) thick. Using a 4-inch (10-cm) round cutter, cut out as many rounds from the dough as possible. If needed, gather together the dough scraps, press together, reroll, and cut out more rounds until you have a total of 8 rounds. Cover the rounds with plastic wrap and repeat with the remaining dough.

Working with 1 round at a time, arrange 1 mound of the filling in the center of the round and brush a little water around the edges of the pastry. Pleat the edges into the middle, covering the filling, and squeeze the edges together gently to seal. Place the pastry, seam side down, on a prepared sheet pan and flatten to form an oval about 2½ inches (6 cm) in diameter. Some of the fruit will be visible through the dough; try not to let it poke through the surface. Brush with a little of the egg white, sprinkle with the Demerara sugar (if using), and cut three slits in the top. Repeat with the remaining dough rounds and filling, arranging the cakes about 1½ inches (4 cm) apart on the prepared pan.

Bake the cakes until they are deep golden brown, 22–25 minutes. Let cool on the pan on a wire rack for at least 10 minutes before serving. Serve warm or at room temperature. The cakes are best when served the same day. They can be reheated in a preheated 300°F (150°C) oven, if desired.

YORKSHIRE TARTS

Traditionally, the custard filling in these tarts was made from curds left over from cheese making. If you are making the creamy curds from scratch, begin a day or two in advance to allow time for them to drain. A specialty of Yorkshire, where *Downton Abbey* is set, these tarts are a shining addition to a teatime table.

FOR THE FILLING

1½ cups (385 g) Homemade Curd Cheese (facing page) or store-bought whole-milk ricotta cheese or cottage cheese

4 tablespoons (60 g) unsalted butter, at room temperature

⅓ cup (70 g) sugar

1 whole egg

1 egg yolk

¾ teaspoon grated lemon zest

¼ cup (35 g) dried currants

Pinch of ground nutmeg

FOR THE PASTRY

1 cup (125 g) flour

3 tablespoons confectioners' sugar

¼ teaspoon salt

6 tablespoons (90 g) cold unsalted butter, cut into 8 pieces, plus room-temperature butter for the muffin cups

1 egg yolk, lightly whisked

Unsalted butter, for the muffin pan

MAKES 10 TARTS

To begin making the filling, prepare the curd cheese as directed. If using store-bought ricotta or cottage cheese, place a fine-mesh sieve over a bowl and spoon the cheese into the sieve. Cover and refrigerate to drain for at least 8 hours or up to overnight.

To make the pastry, in a food processor, combine the flour, confectioners' sugar, and salt and process until blended, about 5 seconds. Scatter the butter pieces over the flour mixture and pulse until the flour mixture forms coarse crumbs, 1–2 minutes. Drizzle the egg over the flour mixture and pulse just until the dough forms moist crumbs, about 10 seconds. Pour the crumbs onto a sheet of plastic wrap, cover with the wrap, and shape into a disk. Refrigerate for at least 30 minutes or up to overnight.

Lightly butter the bottom and sides of 10 standard muffin cups and line the bottom of each cup with parchment paper. Divide the dough into 10 equal pieces (1 slightly rounded tablespoon/20 g each) and roll each piece into a ball. Working with 1 ball at a time and using a lightly floured thumb, gently press the dough onto the bottom and up the sides of a prepared cup, stopping to within ⅛ inch (3 mm) of the rim. Repeat with the remaining dough balls. Cover the pan and refrigerate for at least 20 minutes or up to overnight.

Position a rack in the lower third of the oven and preheat the oven to 375°F (190°C).

To make the filling, in a bowl, using an electric mixer, beat together the drained cheese, butter, and sugar on medium speed until well blended and smooth, 2–3 minutes. Add the whole egg, egg yolk, and lemon zest and beat until just blended, 30–60 seconds. Using a wooden spoon, stir in the currants until evenly distributed.

HOMEMADE CURD CHEESE

6 cups (1.4 l) milk

¼ teaspoon salt

**3 tablespoons fresh
lemon juice**

RECIPE NOTE

The recipe for homemade
curd cheese yields
about 1¾ cups (450 g).
If pressed for time,
use store-bought
whole-milk ricotta
cheese or cottage
cheese; it will still
need to be drained
for at least 8 hours.

Spoon the custard into the tart shells, dividing it evenly (about ¼ cup/60 g each). Top each tart with a touch of nutmeg. Bake the tarts until the filling is puffed and jiggles slightly when the pan is nudged and the crust is golden brown, 21–23 minutes. Let cool completely in the pan on a wire rack. Run a thin-bladed knife between the tart and the cup to loosen each tart, then cover the pan and refrigerate until chilled, 1–2 hours.

To serve, carefully invert the muffin pan onto a large cutting board, releasing the tarts. Transfer the tarts, custard side up, to a large serving plate or individual plates.

To prepare the curd cheese, in a large stainless-steel pot, stir together the milk and salt. Place over medium heat and bring to a boil, stirring occasionally and regularly scraping down the sides and across the bottom of the pan to prevent scorching. When the milk is at a boil, slide the pot off the heat, add the lemon juice, and stir until the mixture begins to separate, about 1 minute. Let stand for 15 minutes.

Place a large fine-mesh sieve over a large bowl and line with a double layer of cheesecloth. Ladle the milk curds and liquid (whey) into the lined sieve. Set aside for 1–2 hours to drain, emptying the whey from the bowl as needed, until most of the liquid has drained out and the cheese is drier and firmer. Cover the bowl-and-sieve setup and refrigerate overnight. The next day, use the cheese immediately, or spoon into a container, cover, and refrigerate for up to 3 days.

RASPBERRY CUSTARD CAKE

Bursting with the flavor of fresh raspberries and vanilla custard, this simple one-layer cake boasts a moist and tender texture. It is perfect at teatime, of course, but it is also welcome as a finish to lunch or dinner.

FOR THE CUSTARD

3 egg yolks

3 tablespoons granulated sugar

Pinch of salt

¾ cup (180 ml) milk

¼ cup (60 ml) heavy cream

1 teaspoon pure vanilla extract or vanilla bean paste

FOR THE CAKE

¾ cup (170 g) unsalted butter, at room temperature, plus more for the pan

1¾ cups (220== g) flour, plus more for the pan

1½ teaspoons baking powder

½ teaspoon salt

1 cup (200 g) granulated sugar

3 eggs, at room temperature

1½ teaspoons pure vanilla extract

1½ cups (170 g) raspberries

2 tablespoons sliced almonds, toasted

Confectioners' sugar, for dusting

SERVES 8–12

To make the custard, in a saucepan, whisk together the egg yolks, granulated sugar, and salt until blended and lighter in color, about 1 minute. Pour in the milk and cream and whisk until blended, about 30 seconds. Place over medium-low heat and cook, stirring constantly, until the mixture is thick enough to coat the back of a spoon and hold a line drawn through it with your finger, 4–5 minutes. (It should register 170°F/77°C on an instant-read thermometer.) Remove from the heat, add the vanilla, and whisk until blended. Scrape into a small bowl and let cool to room temperature, then cover and refrigerate until cold, 2–3 hours or up to 2 days. For faster cooling, set the bowl over a larger bowl filled with ice and water and stir until cold. You should have 1¼ cups (310 g).

To make the cake, preheat the oven to 350°F (180°C). Lightly butter the bottom and sides of a 10-inch (25-cm) square cake pan or a 10-inch (25-cm) round springform pan, then dust with flour, tapping out the excess.

Have the cold custard ready. In a small bowl, whisk together the flour, baking powder, and salt. In a large bowl, using an electric mixer, beat the butter on medium speed until smooth, about 1 minute. Increase the speed to medium-high, add the sugar, and beat until fluffy and lighter in color, 2–3 minutes. Add the eggs, one at a time, beating well after each addition and adding the vanilla with the final egg. On low speed, add half the flour mixture and mix just until blended, then add half of the custard and mix just until blended. Add the remaining flour mixture and again mix just until blended.

Transfer the batter to the prepared pan, spread evenly, and smooth the top. Scatter the berries over the batter, drizzle the remaining custard on top, and finish with the sliced almonds. Bake the cake until a toothpick inserted into the center comes out clean, 43–45 minutes. Let cool in the pan on a wire rack for at least 20 minutes. Serve warm.

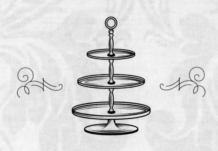

TEA SANDWICHES
& SAVORY BITES

MINI PORK PIES

Traditionally made with a heavy lard-infused dough, these savory mini pies instead use a butter-and-shortening crust. The result is a lighter, flakier, and more flavorful pastry. The quail egg is optional but a fun addition. If you're not using the egg, the pies will be slightly less full. Either way, Mrs. Patmore would surely approve.

FOR THE PASTRY

2½ cups (320 g) flour, plus more for the work surface

¾ teaspoon salt

½ cup (115 g) cold unsalted butter, diced

¼ cup (60 g) cold solid vegetable shortening, diced

⅓ cup (80 ml) very cold water

2 teaspoons fresh lemon juice

FOR THE FILLING

8 quail eggs (optional)

1 lb (450 g) ground pork

6 slices bacon (4 oz/115 g), chopped

3 tablespoons finely diced yellow onion

1 teaspoon salt

½ teaspoon dried thyme or sage (optional)

Good pinch of ground nutmeg (optional)

Good pinch of black pepper

FOR ASSEMBLY

Unsalted butter, for the muffin cups

2 teaspoons unseasoned fine dried bread crumbs

1 egg, lightly whisked

MAKES 8 PIES

To make the pastry, in a food processor, combine the flour and salt and process until blended, about 5 seconds. Scatter the butter and shortening over the flour mixture and process briefly until the butter is coated with flour and slightly chopped, about 2 seconds. Sprinkle the water and lemon juice over the flour mixture and process until the dough comes together in small, moist crumbs, 7–10 seconds.

Scrape the dough onto a lightly floured work surface and shape into a thick rectangle, then divide into 2 pieces, one twice as large as the other. Wrap in storage wrap and refrigerate until well chilled, about 2 hours or up to overnight. You should have about 1¼ lb (570 g) dough.

To make the filling, if using the quail eggs, fill a saucepan three-fourths full with water and bring to a boil over high heat. Gently lower the eggs into the water and cook for 2 minutes. Using a slotted spoon, transfer the eggs to a bowl of ice water to stop the cooking. While the eggs are still warm, carefully peel away the shells. Set the eggs aside, or cover and refrigerate for 1 hour or up to overnight.

In a bowl, combine the pork, bacon, onion, salt, thyme (if using), nutmeg (if using), and pepper and mix until well blended. Set aside, or cover and refrigerate for 1 hour or up to overnight.

Line an 11 x 17-inch (28 x 43-cm) sheet pan with aluminum foil. Position a rack in the lower third of the oven, place the foil-lined pan on the rack, and preheat the oven to 425°F (220°C). Lightly butter the bottom and sides of 8 standard muffin cups, then line the bottoms with parchment paper.

To assemble the pies, on a lightly floured work surface, roll out the larger portion of pastry ⅛ inch (3 mm) thick. Cut out 8 rounds each 4¾ inches (12 cm) in diameter. If necessary, gather up the scraps, press together, reroll, and cut out more rounds to total 8 rounds.

RECIPE NOTE

Any chunky sausage, such
as breakfast or a sweet
Italian (use
1¼ lb/570 g), is a good
substitute for the
pork-bacon mixture.

Cover the rounds with storage wrap to prevent drying. On the lightly floured work surface, roll out the smaller portion of pastry ⅛ inch (3 mm) thick. Cut out 8 rounds each 3 inches (7.5 cm) in diameter, repeating the gathering and rerolling if necessary. Cut out a ½-inch (12-mm) round from the center of each 3-inch (7.5-cm) round. Cover the rounds to prevent drying.

Line the prepared muffin cups with the larger rounds, pressing each round into the bottom and up the sides. Scatter the bread crumbs in the pastry-lined cups, dividing the crumbs evenly. If using the quail eggs, spoon half of the pork mixture into the cups, dividing it evenly and pressing gently to fill the bottom and to make a shallow well in the center. Arrange a quail egg in each well and top with an equal amount of the remaining filling, doming the mixture slightly in the center. If not using the quail eggs, fill each cup with an equal amount of the meat mixture, doming the mixture slightly in the center. You'll use a total of about ⅓ cup (70 g) of the meat mixture in each cup. Brush the inside edges of the dough with some of the beaten egg. Top each cup with a smaller pastry round, pinch the bottom and top pastries together, and roll the pressed edges inward to seal completely. Brush the tops with more beaten egg.

Reduce the oven temperature to 400°F (200°C). Place the muffin pan on the prepared sheet pan and bake the pies until they are deep golden brown, 40–43 minutes. Transfer the sheet pan to a wire rack and let the pies cool for 10 minutes. Run a thin-bladed knife between each pie and the cup sides to loosen the pie from the pan, then remove the pies from the pan.

Serve the pies warm or at room temperature. The pies are best when served the same day they are baked. They can be reheated in a 300°F (150°C) oven, if desired.

GOUGÈRES

The small, light, and airy *gougère* of the afternoon tea tray is rooted in Burgundy, where it first appeared in the seventeenth century and continues to be the preferred accompaniment to wine tasting in the local cellars. These pastries grew in prominence in the nineteenth century, spreading beyond central France and taking on new flavorings. But traditional cooks kept their classic composition of alpine cheese (typically Gruyère, Comté, or Emmentaler) and rich butter-and-egg choux pastry—a formula that would be put to work in the Downton kitchen.

2 cups (480 ml) plus 2 tablespoons milk

½ cup (115 g) unsalted butter

2 teaspoons salt

2 cups (250 g) flour

8 eggs

½ lb (225 g) Gruyère, Emmentaler, or other Swiss-type cheese, finely shredded

MAKES ABOUT 48 PUFFS

Preheat the oven to 375°F (190°C). Line two sheet pans with parchment paper.

In a heavy saucepan over high heat, combine 2 cups (480 ml) of the milk, the butter, and salt and bring to a boil. Add the flour all at once, reduce the heat to low, and stir until the mixture forms a ball and pulls cleanly away from the sides of the pan, about 5 minutes. Remove from the heat and let cool for 2 minutes.

Using an electric mixer on medium speed, add the eggs, one at a time, beating well after each addition until thoroughly incorporated and the dough is very shiny; this step should take about 5 minutes. Stir in three-fourths of the cheese.

Using a spoon, scoop out rounds 2–3 inches (5–7.5 cm) in diameter onto the prepared sheet pans, spacing them about 2 inches (5 cm) apart. Brush the rounds with the remaining 2 tablespoons milk, then sprinkle evenly with the remaining cheese.

Bake the pastries until well puffed and golden brown, 30–35 minutes. Let the pastries cool briefly on the pans on wire racks and serve warm, or let cool completely and serve at room temperature.

CHEESE BOUCHÉES

Bouchée, literally "mouthful," is a French pastry with a savory or sweet filling. According to legend, these rich, flaky pastries were created in the palace kitchen of Louis XV at the request of Queen Marie and made their way to the finest tables of neighboring Britain, as evidenced by Alfred's making a batch of them in season 4 of *Downton.* Bouchées vary in size, with the smaller ones suitable for serving as an *amuse-bouche,* an hors d'oeuvre, a canapé, or a tasty offering on the afternoon tea tray.

FOR THE PASTRY

1⅓ cups (165 g) flour,
plus more for the work surface

6 tablespoons (90 g) cold salted
butter, cut into small cubes

4–5 tablespoons (60–75 ml)
ice-cold water

FOR THE FILLING

1 egg

¼ cup (30 g) grated sharp
Cheddar cheese

¼ cup (30 g) grated Parmesan
cheese

1 tablespoon salted butter,
melted and cooled

Pinch of cayenne pepper
(optional)

Salt and black pepper

Milk, for sealing and brushing

MAKES ABOUT
20 BOUCHÉES

To make the pastry, put the flour into a bowl, scatter the butter over the top, and work the butter into the flour with a pastry blender or your fingertips until the mixture is the consistency of bread crumbs. Add just enough of the water, stirring and tossing the flour mixture with a fork as you do, until the dough comes together in a rough mass. Shape into a ball, wrap in storage wrap, and refrigerate for 20–30 minutes.

To make the filling, in a bowl, whisk the egg until blended. Add both cheeses, the butter, cayenne (if using), and a little salt and black pepper and mix well.

Preheat the oven to 400°F (200°C). Line a sheet pan with parchment paper.

Divide the dough in half. Re-cover and refrigerate half. On a lightly floured work surface, roll out the other half into a round about ¹⁄₁₆ inch (2 mm) thick. Using a 3½-inch (9-cm) round cutter, cut out as many rounds as possible. To shape each pastry, put about ¾ teaspoon of the filling on half of a dough round, leaving the edge uncovered. Brush the entire edge of the round with milk, then fold

MRS. HUGHES: *I have a confession.*
I let them have their tea in my sitting room.

CARSON: *That was nice of you.*

MRS. HUGHES: *It was quite nice. But I had my reasons.*
There's a grating on the wall which means you can hear
what's being said in the room.

~ SEASON 2, EPISODE I

the uncovered half over the filling to form a half-moon, pressing the edges to seal. Bring the corners together and press firmly, sealing them well (like shaping tortellini). Transfer the filled pastries to the prepared pan and refrigerate them while you roll out, fill, and shape the remaining dough.

Arrange all the filled pastries on the pan, spacing them about 1½ inches (4 cm) apart. Lightly brush the tops with milk. Bake the pastries until golden brown, 22–24 minutes. Let the pastries cool briefly on the pan on a wire rack and serve warm, or let cool completely and serve at room temperature.

CORNISH PASTIES

Few foods have a greater regional history than the pasty, a minced meat pie that dates from medieval times but became particularly common in the sixteenth century as a simple meal for tin miners in rural Cornwall. A miner could easily transport the pasty (usually filled with vegetables rather than more costly meat) to work, keep it warm in the mine, and eat it without utensils. If the pasty grew cold, the miner would place it on a shovel and warm it over a fire. The basic pasty recipe survived into the Edwardian era, where its appeal as an accompaniment to afternoon tea—depending on its size and on the refinement of its filling and its pastry—reached across the classes.

FOR THE PASTRY

4½ cups (560 g) all-purpose flour, plus more for the work surface

1¼ teaspoons salt

7½ oz (210 g) suet, solid vegetable shortening, or salted butter, shredded or cut into bits

1 cup plus 2 tablespoons (270 ml) cold water

MAKES 12 PASTIES

To make the pastry, in a large bowl, combine the flour, salt, and suet and quickly mix with your fingertips until the mixture resembles coarse crumbs. Using a pastry blender or a fork, mix in the water, a little at a time, until the mixture is evenly moistened and can be formed into a ball. Divide the dough in half and pat each half into a disk. Wrap each disk in plastic wrap and refrigerate while you make the filling.

To make the filling, in a bowl, combine the apples, pork, bacon, Worcestershire sauce, and sage and stir to mix well. Season with salt and pepper.

Preheat the oven to 375°F (190°C). Line a sheet pan with parchment paper.

On a generously floured work surface, roll out 1 dough disk about ⅛ inch (3 mm) thick. Using a saucer as a guide, cut out 6 circles each about 6 inches (15 cm) in diameter. (If needed, gather up the dough scraps, press together, reroll, and cut out more circles until you have 6 circles.) Divide half of the filling evenly among the circles,

FOR THE FILLING

2 small apples, such as Granny Smith or Cox's Orange Pippin, peeled, halved, cored, and cut into ½-inch (12-mm) cubes

7 oz (200 g) boneless pork shoulder, trimmed of excess fat and cut into ½-inch (12-mm) cubes

¼ lb (115 g) bacon, minced

1 tablespoon Worcestershire sauce

1 teaspoon dried sage, or 1 tablespoon minced fresh sage

Salt and black pepper

spooning it onto half of each circle and leaving ½ inch (12 mm) uncovered around the edge. With a fingertip, dampen the edge of each circle with water, fold the circles in half, and press down on the edge to seal. Crimp the edges with a fork or with your fingers then fold or roll the end corners underneath. Prick the tops several times with a fork to vent and arrange on the prepared sheet pan, spacing them well apart. Repeat with the remaining pastry and filling.

Bake the pasties until barely golden on top and a thermometer inserted into the center of a pasty registers 165°F (74°C), about 20 minutes. Transfer to a wire rack to cool. Serve warm or at room temperature.

ROBERT: *As usual our expectations are disappointed. Let's have some tea.*

~ SEASON 3, EPISODE 8

TEA SANDWICHES

With lunch at noon and dinner at eight, the afternoon tea proved the perfect answer to snacking politely before mealtime, and small, delicate finger sandwiches played a big role in quelling late-afternoon hunger. Custom dictated the sandwiches be made with two thin, crustless slices of bread. The filling was most commonly butter, mayonnaise, or cream cheese and paper-thin vegetable slices, or flavorful combinations like Cheddar cheese and pickle relish and ham and English mustard, though the offerings went beyond these classics.

CUCUMBER

¾ English cucumber

Salt

8 thin slices good-quality white bread, such as pain de mie

Unsalted butter, at room temperature

White pepper

SERVES 4–6

Slice the cucumber as thinly as possible. Put the slices into a colander in the sink or into a sieve over a bowl, sprinkle lightly with salt, and let stand for 20 minutes. Taste a slice to make sure you haven't added too much salt. If you discover you have, rinse the slices briefly under cool running water. Lay a few paper towels on a work surface, arrange the cucumber slices in a single layer on the towels, and pat the slices dry.

Lay the bread slices on a work surface and spread each slice generously with butter. Arrange the cucumber slices, overlapping them, on 4 of the bread slices and sprinkle with pepper. Top with the remaining bread slices, buttered side down.

Using a serrated knife, cut off the crusts from each sandwich, then cut the sandwiches into neat fingers, triangles, or quarters.

Recipe continues on the following page

TEA ETIQUETTE

Today, triangle-shaped sandwiches are fashionable, but in the Edwardian era, sandwiches were commonly rectangular. The crusts should always be trimmed off, then the sandwiches cut into the desired shape and neatly stacked.

Continued

DEVILED EGG & CRESS

4 eggs

4 tablespoons (60 g) unsalted butter, at room temperature

¼ cup (60 ml) mayonnaise

1 teaspoon finely chopped fresh parsley

½ teaspoon finely chopped fresh dill

⅛ teaspoon grated lemon zest

Salt and black pepper

Sweet paprika

8 slices good-quality white bread, such as pain de mie

½ cup (15 g) watercress leaves

SERVES 4–6

In a heavy saucepan, combine the eggs with water to cover by 1–2 inches (2.5–5 cm) and bring to a boil over high heat. Remove from the heat, cover, and let stand for 15 minutes. Transfer the eggs to a bowl of cold water and let stand for 15 minutes to stop the cooking.

Peel the eggs and drop them into a clean bowl. Mash with a fork, then add the butter, mayonnaise, parsley, dill, and lemon zest and mix well. Season to taste with salt, pepper, and paprika.

Lay the bread slices on a work surface. Spread 4 of the slices with the egg mixture, dividing it evenly. Arrange the watercress leaves evenly over the egg mixture. Top with the remaining 4 bread slices and press firmly.

Using a serrated knife, cut off the crusts from each sandwich, then cut the sandwiches into neat fingers, triangles, or quarters.

SMOKED SALMON & DILL

½ lb (225 g) cream cheese, at room temperature

2 tablespoons finely chopped fresh dill

½ lemon

Salt and black pepper

8 slices dense whole-wheat bread

½ lb (225 g) smoked salmon, thinly sliced

SERVES 4–6

In a small bowl, combine the cream cheese and dill and mix with a fork until well blended. Season to taste with lemon juice, salt, and pepper.

Lay the bread slices on a work surface. Spread the seasoned cream cheese on the bread slices, dividing it evenly. Arrange the salmon in an even layer over 4 of the slices, then top with the remaining 4 slices, cream cheese side down.

Using a serrated knife, cut off the crusts from each sandwich, then cut each sandwich into neat fingers, triangles, or quarters.

ROAST BEEF & CHIVE

8 slices good-quality white bread, such as pain de mie

Creamy horseradish, for spreading

8 thin slices roast beef

2 tablespoons minced fresh chives

Salt and black pepper

4 leaves butter lettuce

SERVES 4–6

Lay the bread slices on a work surface. Spread each slice with a thin layer of horseradish. Top 4 of the bread slices with the roast beef slices and the chives, dividing them evenly, and season with salt and pepper. Arrange a lettuce leaf over the roast beef. Top with the remaining 4 bread slices and press firmly.

Using a serrated knife, cut off the crusts from each sandwich, then cut each sandwich into neat fingers, triangles, or quarters.

PRESERVES & SPREADS

QUICK STRAWBERRY JAM

Fruit preserves, particularly berry jams, are a mainstay of the afternoon tea table.
Properly presented in a pretty jar or small china dish, jam in the *Downton* era
would likewise have been accompanied by a designated spoon—usually small, silver,
and ornately embellished with a fruit motif that signaled the flavor in the jam
being served.

**2 pints (700 g) strawberries,
stemmed, cored, and sliced**

1 cup (200 g) sugar

**2 tablespoons fresh
lemon juice**

MAKES ABOUT 3 HALF-PINT
(240-ML) JARS

Place a couple of saucers in the freezer for testing the jam.

In a heavy saucepan over medium heat, combine the strawberries,
sugar, and lemon juice and bring to a boil, stirring constantly until
the sugar dissolves. Reduce the heat to medium-low and cook,
stirring occasionally, until the berries are tender and the juices
thicken, about 10 minutes. To test if the jam is ready, remove a
chilled saucer from the refrigerator, drop a small spoonful of the
jam onto the saucer, and let sit for 30 seconds, then gently nudge
the spoonful. If it wrinkles, the jam is ready. If it doesn't, cook for
1–2 minutes longer and test again with a clean chilled saucer.

Ladle the jam into jars and let cool. Cover and refrigerate for up
to 10 days.

SYBIL: *I only need the basics. How to boil an egg,
how to make tea.*

MRS. PATMORE: *Don't you know how to make tea?*

SYBIL: *Not really.*

~ SEASON 2, EPISODE 1

BLACKBERRY JAM

Some of the hedgerows around the Downton estate would likely have been loaded with blackberries from late July into September, keeping Mrs. Patmore and Daisy busy stirring pots on the stove and then packing the jam into jars for use the rest of the year. At teatime, the jam might be spread on scones or used as a filling for small tarts.

3 quarts (1.7 kg) blackberries

3 cups (600 g) sugar

¾ cup (340 ml) fresh lemon juice

MAKES 6 HALF-PINT (240-ML) JARS

HISTORY NOTE

Estates like Downton produced much of their own food. Jams would typically be homemade, flour might be milled from the estate's own grain, and butter would come from a tenant farm.

Have ready sterilized canning jars and flat lids and screw bands (see Preserving Protocol on page 133). Place a couple of saucers in the freezer for testing the jam.

In a large nonreactive saucepan, gently toss together the berries, sugar, and lemon juice. Bring to a boil over medium-high heat, reduce the heat to medium, and cook uncovered, stirring frequently, until the jam has thickened, about 15 minutes. To test if the jam is ready, remove a chilled saucer from the refrigerator, drop a small spoonful of the jam onto the saucer, and let sit for 30 seconds, then gently nudge the spoonful. If it wrinkles, the jam is ready. If not, return the pan to the heat and boil the jam for 1–2 minutes longer, then test again with a clean chilled saucer. It will continue to thicken as it cools.

Ladle the hot jam into the jars, leaving a ¼-inch (6-mm) headspace. Slide a sterilized metal chopstick or other thin tool down the side of each jar, between the glass and jam, four or five times. This will release any air bubbles. Adjust the headspace, if necessary. Wipe the rims clean and seal tightly with the lids.

Process the jars in a boiling-water bath for 10 minutes. Transfer the jars to a folded towel and let cool completely. Check the seal on each cooled jar by pressing on the center of the lid. If the lid stays down, the seal is good. Store properly sealed jars in a cool, dark place for up to 1 year. Store any jars that failed to seal in the refrigerator for up to 3 weeks.

CURRANT JELLY

Unlike jams, which are thick and spoonable, jellies are smooth, clear spreads from which all of the fruit solids have been strained. Fresh currants are a favorite jelly ingredient, as they naturally possess the perfect amount of pectin and acidity, ensuring both a good gel without the addition of commercial pectin and a color as brilliant as the fruit.

1 lb (450 g) fresh currants

½ cup (120 ml) water

1 cup (200 g) sugar, or as needed

MAKES ONE I PINT (480-ML) JAR

In a large nonreactive saucepan, combine the currants and water. Bring to a boil over medium-high heat, mashing the currants with a wooden spoon or a potato masher to release their juice. Reduce the heat to low and cook uncovered, stirring frequently, until the currants are very soft, about 15 minutes.

Suspend a jelly bag over a deep nonreactive bowl and pour the currant mixture into the bag. Let the bag stand overnight or until all the juice has been expressed. Do not squeeze the bag, or the jelly will be cloudy.

The next day, place a couple of saucers in the freezer for testing the jelly. Remove the bag and discard the solids. Measure the currant juice, pour into a large nonreactive saucepan, and add an equal amount of sugar (or about 1 cup/200 g). Bring to a boil over high heat, reduce the heat to medium-high, and cook uncovered, stirring frequently and skimming off any foam that forms on the surface, until the jelly is thick enough to sheet off the back of a spoon, 10–15 minutes. Remove from the heat. To test if the jelly is ready, remove a chilled saucer from the refrigerator, drop 1 teaspoon of the jelly onto the saucer, and return it to the freezer for 2 minutes. If the mixture wrinkles when nudged gently with a finger, it is ready. If not, return the pan to the heat and boil the jelly for 1–2 minutes longer, then test again with a clean chilled saucer.

Ladle the hot jelly into a jar and let cool. Cover and refrigerate for up to 1 month.

STRAWBERRY-RHUBARB JAM

Strawberries and rhubarb are the long-awaited first sign of spring fruit. Because they are low in pectin, oranges, both the peel and the flesh, are added to give this bright-flavored, tangy jam the body it needs. Set it out with cream scones, biscuits, or crusty bread.

2 oranges, preferably blood oranges

1½–2 lb (680 g–1 kg) rhubarb, cut into ½-inch (12-mm) chunks (about 6 cups)

3 cups (420 g) strawberries, hulled and sliced

4 cups (800 g) sugar

½ cup (120 ml) fresh lemon juice

MAKES 7 HALF-PINT
(240-ML) JARS

Cut a thin slice off both ends of each orange. Cut the oranges in half crosswise and remove and discard the seeds. In a food processor, process the orange halves until roughly puréed. Transfer to a nonreactive bowl. Add the rhubarb, strawberries, and sugar to the oranges and toss gently to combine. Cover and refrigerate for at least 8 hours or up to overnight.

The next day, have ready sterilized canning jars and flat lids and screw bands (see Preserving Protocol on page 133). Place a couple of saucers in the freezer for testing the jam.

Transfer the rhubarb mixture to a large nonreactive saucepan and add the lemon juice. Bring to a boil over medium-high heat, reduce the heat to medium, and cook uncovered, stirring frequently, for 10 minutes. Remove from the heat. To test if the jam is ready, remove a chilled saucer from the refrigerator, drop a small spoonful of the jam onto the saucer, and let sit for 30 seconds, then gently nudge the spoonful. If it wrinkles, the jam is ready. If it doesn't, cook for 1–2 minutes longer and test again with a clean chilled saucer.

Ladle the hot jam into the jars, leaving a ¼-inch (6-mm) headspace. Slide a sterilized metal chopstick or other thin tool down the side of each jar, between the glass and jam, four or five times. This will release any air bubbles. Adjust the headspace, if necessary. Wipe the rims clean and seal tightly with the lids.

Process the jars in a boiling-water bath for 10 minutes. Transfer the jars to a folded towel and let cool completely. Check the seal on each cooled jar by pressing on the center of the lid. If the lid stays down, the seal is good. Store properly sealed jars in a cool, dark place for up to 1 year. Store any jars that failed to seal in the refrigerator for up to 3 weeks.

ORANGE MARMALADE

In Britain, orange marmalade has historically been prepared with bitter Seville orange, and much has been made of putting up the wildly popular preserves—a staple of both the breakfast and the teatime table—during the short Seville orange season. This recipe uses sweet oranges, but any orange variety can be used by varying the amount of sugar depending on the bitterness of the fruit.

2 lb (1 kg) oranges

8 cups (1.9 l) water

Up to 6 cups (1.2 kg) sugar

2 cups (480 ml) fresh orange juice

½ cup (120 ml) fresh lemon juice

MAKES 7 HALF-PINT
(240-ML) JARS

Have ready sterilized canning jars and flat lids and screw bands (see Preserving Protocol, facing page). Place a couple of saucers in the freezer for testing the jam.

Cut a thin slice off both ends of each orange. Slice each orange crosswise as thinly as possible, preferably on a mandoline. In a large, nonreactive saucepan over medium-high heat, combine the orange slices and water and bring to a boil. Cook uncovered, stirring, for 15 minutes. Remove from the heat and let cool slightly.

Measure the orange slices and their liquid and return to the pan. For each 1 cup (240 ml), add ¾ cup (150 g) sugar to the pan. Stir in the orange and lemon juices. Bring to a boil over medium-high heat and boil rapidly for 10 minutes. Reduce the heat to medium and cook, stirring frequently, until slightly thickened and gelatinous, 7–10 minutes longer. Remove from the heat. To test if the marmalade is ready, remove a chilled saucer from the refrigerator, drop a small spoonful of the marmalade onto the saucer, and let sit for 30 seconds, then gently nudge the spoonful. If it wrinkles, the marmalade is ready. If it doesn't, cook for 1–2 minutes longer and test again with a clean chilled saucer.

Ladle the hot marmalade into the jars, leaving a ¼-inch (6-mm) headspace. Slide a metal chopstick or other thin tool down the side of each jar, between the glass and the marmalade, four or five times. This will release any air bubbles. Adjust the headspace, if necessary, then wipe the rims clean and seal tightly with the lids.

Process the jars in a boiling-water bath for 10 minutes. Transfer the jars to a folded towel and let cool completely. Check the seal on each cooled jar by pressing on the center of the lid. If the lid stays down, the seal is good. Store properly sealed jars in a cool, dark place for up to 1 year. Store any jars that failed to seal in the refrigerator for up to 3 weeks.

PRESERVING PROTOCOL

To sterilize jars for holding preserves, first wash the jars with hot, soapy water. Put the clean jars upright in a large pot, add hot water to cover by 2 inches (5 cm), and bring to a boil over high heat. Boil the water for 15 minutes, then turn off the heat. The jars can remain in the hot water for up to 1 hour. Using a jar lifter or tongs, lift out the jars, draining them well, and set aside on a kitchen towel to dry. To sterilize two-part canning lids—rubber-lined lid and screw band—sterilize them in simmering (not boiling) water for 10 minutes.

If a recipe calls for a boiling-water bath, use the same pot and water you used for sterilizing the jars. Put a rack on the bottom of the pot and bring the water to a boil. Using a jar lifter or tongs, lower the filled jars onto the rack, spacing them about ½ inch (12 mm) apart. The water should cover the jars by 2 inches (5 cm); add more boiling water if needed. Bring to a rolling boil, cover, and boil for 10 minutes. Turn off the heat and let the jars sit for about 10 minutes before removing them from the pot and setting them aside to dry.

LEMON CURD

The term *lemon curd* has a long history in British culinary tradition, though its meaning has varied over the years. Early on, it meant literally curds—or cheese—arrived at by adding lemon juice to fresh cream and then separating the curds from the whey. What remains a mystery is when those simple curds became the creamy citrus custard made from lemon juice, eggs, and butter that was served at Downton—and is still served today.

1 whole egg

4 egg yolks

½ cup (100 g) sugar

⅓ cup (80 ml) fresh lemon juice

2 tablespoons unsalted butter, cubed

MAKES ABOUT 1 CUP (250 G)

In a heatproof bowl set over (not touching) barely simmering water in a saucepan, whisk together the whole egg, egg yolks, sugar, and lemon juice. Cook, stirring constantly, until thickened, 5–8 minutes. To test if it is ready, pull the spoon out of the bowl and draw your finger across the back of it; if your finger leaves a trail that does not fill in immediately, the curd is ready.

Remove from the heat and add the butter, stirring until incorporated. Strain through a fine-mesh sieve into another bowl. Cover with plastic wrap, pressing the plastic directly onto the surface of the curd (this helps prevent a skin from forming). Refrigerate until well chilled and set, about 3 hours, before using. The curd will keep in an airtight container in the refrigerator for up to 1 week.

MOCK CLOTTED CREAM

Clotted cream is a requisite component of a proper English cream tea and a classic accompaniment to scones. Prized for its natural thick consistency and mild nutty flavor, it is produced in Devon and Cornwall, where it is known as Devonshire cream and Cornish cream respectively (see page 104). It is made by heating unpasteurized milk until a thick layer of cream forms on its surface and then skimming off the cream layer once the milk has cooled. Although no combination of ingredients can replicate the unique flavor and consistency of true clotted cream, this mock recipe, which mixes mascarpone cheese with heavy cream, is a respectable substitute.

½ cup (120 ml) heavy cream

1 cup (225 g) mascarpone cheese, at room temperature

1 tablespoon confectioners' sugar, or to taste

MAKES ABOUT 1 CUP (250 G)

In a bowl, using an electric mixer, beat the cream on medium-high speed until soft peaks form. On medium speed, add the mascarpone and sugar and beat until incorporated. Taste, then adjust with more sugar if needed. Serve at once.

TEA ETIQUETTE

Both Cornwall and Devon lay claim to the invention of the cream tea, which consists of scones with clotted cream and fruit jams (preserves) served along with the tea. The residents of each county have strong views on the order of the preserves and cream. The Devonshire tradition is cream first with preserves spread on top, while the Cornish tradition is preserves first with the cream on top. For everyone else, the order remains one of personal preference.

weldon**owen**

Publisher **Roger Shaw**
Associate Publisher **Amy Marr**
Creative Director **Chrissy Kwasnik**
Art Director **Bronwyn Lane**
Photography Director & Designer **Lisa Berman**
Managing Editor **Tarji Rodriguez**
Production Manager **Binh Au**

Food Photographer **John Kernick**
Food Stylist **Cyd Raftus McDowell**
Prop Stylist **Suzie Myers**
Cover Illustration **Conor Buckley**

Produced by Weldon Owen International
1150 Brickyard Cove Road
Richmond, CA 94801
www.weldonowen.com

Printed and bound in China

First printed in 2020
10 9 8 7 6 5 4 3 2 1

Library of Congress Cataloging-in-Publication
data is available.

ISBN: 978-1-68188-503-2

INTRODUCTORY TEXT BY **REGULA YSEWIJN**

**WELDON OWEN WISHES TO THANK
THE FOLLOWING PEOPLE FOR THEIR
GENEROUS SUPPORT IN PRODUCING THIS BOOK**

Julian Fellowes, Rizwan Alvi, Lisa Atwood, Antoinette Cardoza, Manuel Cardoza,
Abigail Dodge, Mimi Freund, Annie Gray, Charlotte Havelange, Rachel Markowitz,
Elizabeth Parson, Nico Sherman, Sharon Silva, and Josh Simons

CARNIVAL FILMS
Gareth Neame, Aliboo Bradbury, Charlotte Fay, and Nion Hazell

PETERS FRASER AND DUNLOP
Annabel Merullo and Laura McNeill